ROCK BOTTOM

ROCK BOTTOM

the book of pop atrocities

MUCK RAKER

Proteus Books

PROTEUS BOOKS is an imprint of
The Proteus Publishing Group

United States
PROTEUS PUBLISHING CO., INC
733 Third Avenue
New York, N Y 10017

distributed by
THE SCRIBNER BOOK COMPANIES, INC
597, Fifth Avenue
New York, N Y 10017

United Kingdom
PROTEUS (PUBLISHING) LIMITED
Bremar House,
Sale Place,
London, W2 1PT

ISBN 0 906071 79 8

First published in 1981
© 1981 M. Raker and Proteus (Publishing) Ltd
All rights reserved

Printed in Great Britain by
The Anchor Press Ltd., Tiptree, Essex
Bound by William Brendon & Son Ltd
Tiptree, Essex

CONTENTS

YOU NAME IT
artists and bands

page 9

SINGULARLY PAINFUL
singles and EPs

page 31

SELF-WORSHIP MADE SIMPLE
the ego page

page 44

TORTURE AT 33^{1}3
albums

page 46

MEET THE PUBLIC
on tour and in performance

page 64

THE WORST...
of the best and the worst of the rest

page 77

RECORD SLEEVE SLEAZE
cover art to forget

page 96

ALL YOU NEED IS HYPE
promotion and advertising

page 114

CRUSHED BEATLES
the fab four dismembered

page 126

CARELESS TALK
quotes outrageous and unfortunate

page 128

DRUGS AND OTHER JUNK
paraphernalia

page 138

INTRODUCTION

It isn't easy to verbalize the feelings of someone who has lived and breathed Rock 'n' Roll from the beginning, but whose current sentiments verge on suicidal despair. Once upon a time, rock really seemed to be the answer to the mounting frustrations of a young, post-war world looking for something new, but now it's getting to the point where the music's no longer the answer but part of the problem.

In the 1950s and 60s, even as recently as '77, rock music was fun, an exciting and stimulating industry to be involved in, but strictly fun. 'The industry of Human Happiness', Andrew Loog Oldham, erstwhile manager of the Rolling Stones, used to call it. In the 1980s it's become more like the industry of human gloom, a mess of drugs, death, disagreements and doom. And a bunch of people running around taking things so damn *seriously*. There would have been no point in writing a book like this during the halcyon days of rock – expressing sympathy for the odd musician who couldn't cope with the pressures of the business would have been more appealing. But nowadays the music scene seems to be populated by fools, this writer among them, and the time is right to burst a few bubbles. A lot of the material included in this survey of rock atrocities is amusing, even hilarious (for which we have to thank the unintentioned efforts of stars as diverse as The Beatles and Auntie Pus), but there's enough that's bizarre, sick or plain idiotic to make you want to weep.
Or perhaps we're all just getting old.

M Raker
July 1981

50
UNNECESSARILY TASTELESS GROUP NAMES

Afflicted Man	The Balls	Blind Drunk
Bouncers International	The Coil	Criminal Class
The Diks	Discharge	The Drug Addix
The Four Skins	The Germs	God's Toys
Invisible Sex	Juan Foot 'n' The Grave	Teenage Jesus and the Jerks
London S.S.	Mean Street Dealers	Marital Aids
Mental As Anything	Molesters	Newtown Neurotics
Nipple Erectors	Nurse With Wound	Pagan Altar
Peter and the Test Tube Babies	Phallus	The Prats
Prison Life	Auntie Pus	Raped
The Rent Boys	Rikki and the Last Days of Earth	Rubber Johnny
Saigon	SAS	Smack
Snatch	Social Security	Solid Waste
Spics	Thief	Theatre of Hate
Thieves Like Us	Those Naughty Lumps	Tools
The Vicars	Victim	The Viletones
The Wimps	The Worst	

YOU NAME IT – artists and bands

As will be abundantly clear from

other parts of this volume, all too often the names of groups, the titles of songs, and even names of record companies are chosen with little regard for common decency, usually on the premise that a particularly lurid name may attract some kind of publicity, even if, in most cases, it is the worst kind. But then any publicity, as oldtime hustlers will tell you, is good publicity . . . and just to underline the point that there are wild and irrational imaginations abroad thinking up stupidly offensive names, consider the following: an American 'comedian' known as Uncle Dirty, a British rock 'n' roll revivalist who called himself Nick Satan (and swore that it was his real name), an American band known as Smegma (for the uninitiated, this is a secretion commonly found between the foreskin and the main shaft of the male member). In the song line, we have a sensitive ditty titled *99% Is Shit* by the Cash Pussies, *Piss Factory* by Patti Smith, or one of the bizarre LPs by San Francisco masked group, The Residents, which they thoughtfully titled *Third Reich 'n' Roll*. As far as record company titles go, how does C.U.N.T. Records of West 29th Street, New York City, grab you?

Nevertheless, the name which should win the prize as being the least tasteful ever is that of The Moors Murderers. The reference is to the crimes committed by Myra Hindley and Ian Brady, on the surface an ordinary typist and clerk who lived together, but whose secret passion was to murder people, especially young children, bury them on the Moorland in the Midlands near where they lived in Britain and picnic on the newly dug graves of their victims. Quite properly, both Brady and Hindley were given life sentences, and it would have been perfectly just and appropriate if this disgusting duo were never heard of again. Unfortunately, there exists a well meaning but ultimately misguided aristocrat named Lord Longford, a man who has been an ardent campaigner for prison reforms of various types. In the case of Myra Hindley, Lord Longford became acquainted with her during one of his prison visits, and became inexplicably

Steve Strange of Visage

convinced that Ms. Hindley was a changed person, who had totally repented of her crimes and should, in Longford's opinion, be given the chance to regain a place in normal society. That this has not yet happened (and hopefully never will) is one of the few positive items in this story. . .

An eighteen year old Welsh boy, now better known as Steve Strange, perhaps the leading figure in the 1981 art/glam rock movement and leader of a group he calls Visage, whose other members are concurrently in other well known bands like Ultravox and Magazine, had been captivated by the music and image of the Sex Pistols when they played a concert in his hometown of Newport, Monmouthshire. Having been well and truly bitten by the rock 'n' roll bug during 1977 Strange moved to London (where the streets are paved with gold, etc.) and became involved with a group of Sex Pistols fans known as the Bromley Contingent (whose members, incidentally, included Siouxsie, leader of the Banshees, and Billy Idol of Generation X). Bursting to become a star, Steve was approached by the legendary figure with the big cigar who told Steve he had potential as a pop singer, but would have to do exactly what he was told, after which his name would very shortly be on everyone's lips. That was one of the few accurate statements made at that point — the unnamed entrepreneur persuaded Steve to front a group to be called The Moors Murderers, and within days of the starstruck Welsh adolescent having agreed, the national newspapers (and to a lesser extent, the music press) were featuring shock/horror headlines proclaiming this latest and even more depraved aspect of the punk rock movement.

In Strange's defense, his ignorance of the unpleasant and devious ways of the music world, due both to his youth and his comparatively brief exposure to the joys and depravities of London, made him a very suitable target for the devious mind of the man who could no doubt claim to have 'discovered' him. However, this is hardly an excuse for the fact that the group indulged in a certain amount of advance publicity, submitting to an interview with one of the music papers in which they allowed themselves to be photographed wearing plastic trashcan liner masks (in retrospect, not such a bad move) and to utter some astoundingly trite quotes: "We're deadly serious about the group name. We've written a song called *Free Hindley*, although what I really mean in the song is that she should be considered for parole".

The group, a quartet, decided that their names were Steve Brady (aka Strange), Vince and John Kray (allegedly brothers of Ronald Kray, another extremely famous and violent British criminal) and Christine Hindley (Steve's girlfriend, it was said). This last individual undoubtedly regrets her involvement in the project at least as much as Strange, as she turned out to be Chrissie Hynde, now world famous as the highly talented leader of her own group, The Pretenders. Just

Chrissie Hynde of The Pretenders

how Ms. Hynde became involved in the interview has never been made clear, as her involvement was supposedly brief and came about because she had agreed to assist the rest of the group with the recording of some audition tapes. It was perhaps unfortunate that she too was unable to realize that the whole concept of a group calling themselves The Moors Murderers was doomed not only to failure but also to utter notoriety courtesy of the gutter press. If there's a lesson to be learned from this (the 'group' fortunately disintegrated very soon after the press furore), it's that such a thing as bad publicity definitely exists, and that the streets of London are also paved with sharks eager to take advantage of photogenic innocents in the hope that they can support the shark's disgusting habits for a few weeks.

Outrage is a weapon which can,

of course, lead to a would be rock act becoming a household name (Harpic?). The most notorious group name, to take but one facet of outrage, is that of The Sex Pistols, an overly polite method of indicating some connection with the male phallus. The Pistols were not alone in the outrageous name stakes during the heydey of British punk rock in the latter half of the 1970s, and among their like-thinking contemporaries were such groups as The Damned (whose drummer rejoices in the pseudonym 'Rat Scabies'), The Stranglers, The Drones, The Slits (one to which a certain very popular British Sunday newspaper took such a violent and somewhat incongruous dislike, considering the atrocities they regularly feature, that it refused to actually publish the group's name – at the time, The Slits were an all-girl group by the way) and a group whose name was obviously intended to be thought of in 'double entendre' terms, The Members.

There were plenty more dubious names during the

Slits

New York Dolls

early punk days, including The Vibrators and the decidedly unpleasant Throbbing Gristle, and the majority of the groups mentioned here did in fact succeed in penetrating the public consciousness to a greater or less extent, although one famous group of the era, Sham 69, whose name was originally presumed to have sexual connotations, was actually in no way related to matters of that nature. It was in fact an abbreviation of some graffiti commemorating a soccer team's success during 1969, when Walton and Hersham, an amateur team, apparently enjoyed a particularly rewarding year. Much of the graffiti had worn away by the time the members of the group were looking for a name, all that remained being 'Sham 69'. Very disappointing to the group's numerous detractors. . .

The more recent heavy metal boom produced its own crop of unsavory names, including Iron Maiden (originally a torture device used in the Middle Ages), Judas Priest, a name which gives a nagging feeling of unpleasantness rather than direct nausea, something which certain critics might suggest can be easily left to the group's music, and another example of the use to which ambiguity can be put, AC/DC. Of the latter, it should perhaps be remembered that the group was formed in Australia. . .

American New Wave rockers soon caught on in the wake of the English punks – Richard Hell and the Voidoids, whose theme tune was titled *(We Belong To The) Blank Generation*, The Dead Boys, whose publicity photographs made their name look most appropriate and the exceedingly obnoxious Teenage Jesus and the Jerks, whose erstwhile lead singer, Lydia Lunch, was reported on several occasions in the music press as enjoying life to its fullest when she and her husband were inflicting very visible wounds on each other. This is a topic to which we will return (the names, that is, rather than the flagellation).

Prefacing a group name with the

word 'Dead' became a popular route towards infamy of a certain type during the latter years of the 70's. Mind you, it had to be just 'Dead', not anything else, as a long since forgotten teenybop combo known as the Dead End Kids would no doubt be pleased to testify, wherever they may be. The same no doubt goes for an Irish band who called themselves Dead Fingers Talk, which was probably not a name selected for its outrageousness, but because of its associations with that immensely trendy novelist,

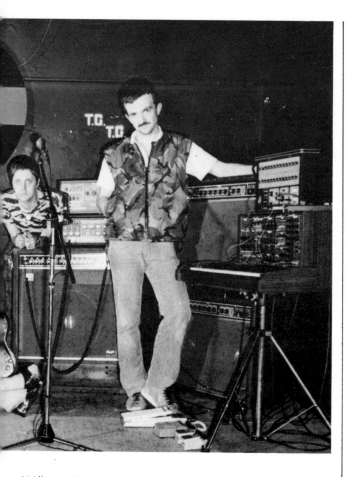

still mentioned in dispatches). Despite the impression that the above may have created, the Dead Boys did record one completely classic track, an epic from their first LP titled *Sonic Reducer*, which remains one of the finest American New Wave tracks of all time. However, the good impression created by this, their first single release (despite certain lyrical drawbacks), was soon dissipated by the subject matter they chose for other songs – *Caught With The Meat In Your Mouth* may charitably sound like an ambiguous title, but from the little that can be discerned of the lyrics, it doesn't seem in the least polite. The second LP, whose tracks included *Flame Thrower Love* and *Son Of Sam* (an individual of this name was caught after having committed numerous unpleasant murders) set an unsavory seal on the group's career. The Dead Kennedys, on the other hand, claim to be much less frivolous about their intentions. Lead singer Jello Biafra maintains: "We're not here to entertain, we're here to annoy. The name's symbolic of the end of the American Dream, and the first Kennedy killing (that of President John Kennedy in 1963) kind of torpedoed the idea that the American Empire was expanding. Ever since then, Americans have become more self-centered than they ever were, to the point where the entire empire they've built is slowly crumbling into little pieces. We figure that one way to bring attention to this state of affairs is by a name like the Dead Kennedys – obviously, it not only symbolizes things, but is a very good bait to suck people in so we can

William Burroughs, who supposedly wrote a book with that title. Leaving the 'dead' prefix aside for a moment, Burroughs inspired at least two better known groups than Dead Fingers Talk, Soft Machine (a reference, apparently, to the human body, and if so, a very poetic one) and the enigmatic American group, now duo, Steely Dan. A steely dan, you may be fascinated to discover, is in fact the nickname given to an obscure type of metal dildo, although this information should probably be concealed from the old or those who are easily shocked.

Reverting to the main topic, two of the more famous groups to use the 'dead' prefix are The Dead Boys and The Dead Kennedys – no prizes for guessing which of the two became the more notorious. The Dead Boys, as is mentioned elsewhere, were not pretty, and their lack of photogenic quality was matched by the titles of their two LPs, the first of which was accurately mirroring the image which the group wanted to portray of themselves – *Young, Loud and Snotty*. Their swan song was equally tasteful, and titled *We Have Come For You Children*, but since its release in 1978, there has been silence from the Dead Boys (and not because they were trying to live up to their epithet, as individual members of the group are

Dead Boys

YOU NAME IT

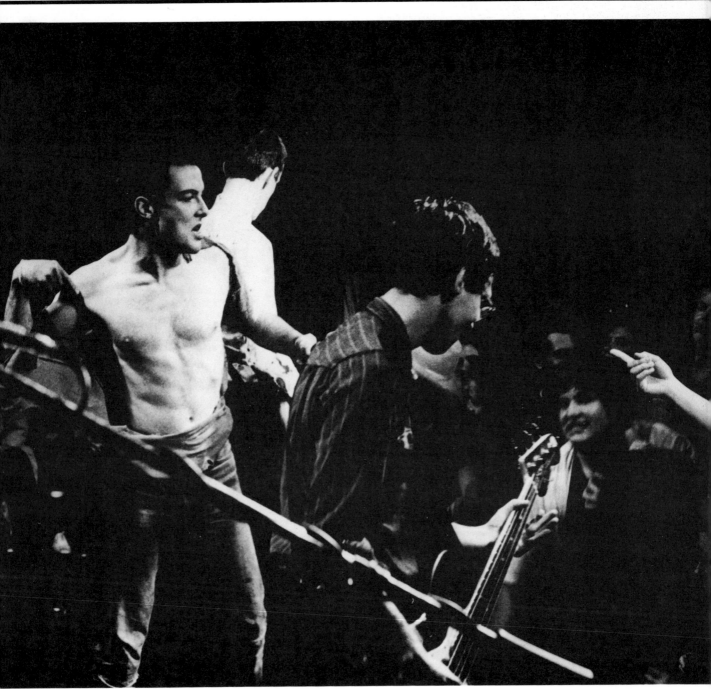

Dead Kennedys

beat them over the head with issues we think they should be aware of, that they refuse to acknowledge". The Dead Kennedys are also at pains to make it clear that what they are doing (frantic 1977 style punk rock but with sarcastic and politically aware lyrics) is meant to be taken seriously: "Anybody who took the time to listen to our records and read more than a line or two of our lyrics would know right away that we don't consider ourselves a joke band. If we were to put the faces of the (famous) Kennedys themselves on our record sleeves, and write about dumb hump-the-secretary jokes and things like that, obviously we'd be a joke band, but we're not".

The earnestness and sincerity of such sentiments (and Mr Biafra has plenty more where they came from) is perhaps a little incongruous when the names

Dead Fingers Talk

of other band members are learned – Jello Biafra is itself an unlikely name, to say the least, while we are probably supposed to learn something from the chosen appellations of bass player Klaus Fluoride and guitarist East Bay Ray Valium. Dead Kennedy's song titles also tend to be a little inflammatory – *California Über Alles, Holiday In Cambodia, I kill Children, Chemical Warfare, Kill The Poor, Ill In The Head* and *Let's Lynch the Landlord*, for example. However, the group's finely tuned sense of outrage is not confined to musical matters – Biafra also ran as a candidate for the post of Mayor of San Francisco, and just how seriously his campaign was regarded by the populace can be understood by the fact that of the ten candidates in the Mayoral race, Biafra polled enough

votes to be placed fourth. One of the major platforms of his campaign was that police officers should have to be elected by the citizens whose area each officer would patrol, and would have to stand for re-election on a regular basis. But perhaps the greatest contribution to the general knowledge of everyday people to which the Dead Kennedys can lay claim (and this is deadly serious) relates to a song whose title has already been mentioned, *Kill the Poor*, whose subject matter revolves around the concept of an advanced nuclear device, the neutron bomb, the effect of which is apparently to destroy life while leaving inanimate objects, like buildings, completely untouched. If that's not an utterly sick concept, then maybe Hitler got it right after all. . .

c. John McKenzie

CAPTAIN BEEFHEART (Né Pon Van Vliet)

is without any doubt an individual of a unique type. To those who enjoy his music, he appears as close to a Messiah, while to those who are unable or unwilling to understand the sound which he and his band members produce, he appears totally and even at times dangerously mad. A few little gems of the Beefheart philosophy may give you the idea: "There are forty people in the world, and five of them are hamburgers". Or how about "Progress is Chanel No. 6 on the rocks"? There's even a distinct similarity with something Kevin Ayers once said "I'm like a woman. I have my periods which give me the cramps every one in a while, and I do something far out".

A famous record producer who shall remain nameless was once asked in an interview about Beefheart's frequent boast that he totally instructed his backing musicians what they should play. "Oh yes, he was proud of that. He'd say 'These guys aren't musicians, they're animals'. He claimed that he used to make sure none of the musicians knew how to play an instrument by picking a guy and telling him 'You're a guitarist', handing him a guitar, and the guy wouldn't know a thing about the guitar. Then Beefheart would say 'It doesn't matter – put your fingers anywhere you want. Here's the rhythm you've got to play'. Beefheart always tries to make art".

Another peculiar Beefheart quirk is his invention of names for his backing musicians. On what is probably his most celebrated work, the 1969 double album titled Trout Mask Replica, the backing band consists of Zoot Horn Rollo on 'glass finger guitar' and flute, Antennae Jimmy Semens playing 'steel appendage guitar', The Mascara Snake on bass clarinet and vocal, and Rockette Morton on bass and narration. It seems unlikely that these names would have been given to anyone by their natural parents,

but perhaps their renaming was necessary in order that they should be able to play songs with titles like My Human Gets Me Blues, Pachuco Cadaver and She's Too Much For My Mirror. Beefheart, despite any impression to the contrary which may be given in this book or elsewhere, is undoubtedly a genius, although, as has been said about many highly talented people, the dividing line between genius and lunacy is very narrow. It is not only the man's mind which is capable of exceptional concepts, his voice is also a remarkable instrument, allegedly with a range of four and a half octaves. One recording session, for Beefheart's first LP, Safe As Milk, was nearly abandoned when the Captain's voice destroyed a twelve hundred dollar microphone; eventually the track, Electricity, was finally finished, although without the intensity the artist would have preferred. Generally, though, it's the stories of Beefheart's unconventional behavior which make the papers – Trout Mask Replica, for example, was recorded in his own house, and the Captain requested his record company to hire a tree surgeon who could live in the house while the record was being made, in order to prevent the trees becoming frightened and falling down. The record company refused, of course, but Beefheart hired his own tree specialist to give the neighborhood trees a medical check, and sent the bill to the record company.

The Captain Beefheart legend continues to grow, as the man continues to make records and to be interviewed, but let's close this particular glance at him with a couple more highly quotable quotations. What do you think about "Everybody's colored, or else you wouldn't be able to see them"? Perhaps better is the remark made during a conversation about whether or not human teeth are made of ivory: "Think about the poor rhinoceros. He's in trouble because people think his horn's good for sex, and they grind it up to make sexual potions. We're really lucky no-one's found out our teeth are ivory' ...

A band
which finally achieved

substantial fame in Britain, after many years of toiling up and down the country for peanuts, is Motorhead. Never the most subtle of bands (in fact, that is an Olympic qualifying understatement), during their early years a presumed combination of inability and stimulants of various types prevented the band from even reaching the starting line in the race towards the charts. In 1975, the band somehow contrived to book themselves into the famed Rockfield Studios in Wales, where Dave Edmunds was acting as resident producer. Dave recalls:– "That was insane. I produced about six tracks for them, but then I couldn't take it any longer. They used to work the most incredible hours – I remember they took about twenty one hours to get one guitar right. I went to bed, and came back, and they were still doing it".

Since that time, there can be no doubt that Motorhead (the name, according to group leader Lemmy, is American slang for 'speed freak', and 'speed' is itself slang for certain types of amphetamines) have improved dramatically, although the group's checkered past continues to catch up with them from time to time. One example which was stranger than most came to light during the late 1970s, when an infant prodigy named Paul Inder, at the time only eleven years old but already the possessor of a man-sized publishing contract, appeared at the annual Reading Rock Festival performing some of his repertoire as one of the early acts on the bill. Few had ever heard of him before (or since, actually), so that it was necessary to provide a modicum of information about Paul to satisfy the inquiries of journalists covering the event. Apart from the obvious 'child genius' talk, it was also mentioned that Lemmy (real name Ian Kilmister) was in fact young Inder's father. Initially, this was treated as a less than subtle joke, but when Lemmy was asked whether the story held any water, he confirmed that it was indeed true: "The blanket I was relying on to prevent anything like this happening wouldn't have held any water either", he noted by way of explanation. . .

Detractors of
popular music would have

everyone else believe that those involved in 'The Industry Of Human Happiness', as Andrew Loog Oldham, erstwhile manager of The Rolling Stones called it, are in fact among the most degenerate individuals in the world. This might account for the fact that only detractors of popular music seem unsurprised by a statistic which everyone else finds somewhat staggering – that in the field of popular music, the last twenty years has seen no less than three examples of sex changes. Whether or not the fact that each of these gene reorganizations was from masculine to feminine is significant, it's difficult to judge.

However, the earliest occurrence was that of the notable orchestra leader Wally Stott (his work can be heard on several tracks by Dusty Springfield recorded during the 1960s) who decided that he would feel a lot more at ease as a lady named Angela Morley. Ms. Morley continued to write and to orchestrate, one of her more recent credits being the score for the film *Watership Down* (with the exception, of course, of the enormously successful *Bright Eyes,* a song taken to the top of the hit parade by Art Garfunkel and written by Mike Batt, whose previous biggest claim to fame was as the musical personification of the Wombles).

The next mutant on the list perhaps qualifies only marginally as he/she is better known in the field of classical music, although there have been several involvements for this person in more frivolous fields, and during the peak years of hippiedom, the name of Walter Carlos (one of the first people to successfully experiment with synthesiser music) was synonymous with 'far out' sounds, highly appropriate to a drug-induced stupor. Walter's problem, according to one of his devotees, was that he looked rather more like Faye Dunaway than Walter anyone, and during the 1970s (a period when much of his most highly acclaimed work was produced, including the soundtrack to the film *A Clockwork Orange*), Walter 'had the operation' and emerged as Wendy Carlos, a name apparently far more appropriate to his physical appearance. Little seems to have altered in terms of the Carlos ability – in 1980, Wendy contributed to the score of another Stanley Kubrick film, *The Shining*. The above mentioned devotee of Walter/Wendy also posed an interesting conundrum when supplying some of this information: would the sex change also result in some kind of alteration in Carlos' ability to create original and exceptional music, he wondered, and if so, would the change be for the worse, bearing in mind the widely accepted theory that the best artistic work is done by those afflicted by pain?

Third in the series of boys who wanted to be girls so much that they actually did something about it is Wayne/Jayne County, an American New Wave singer. Always a little dejected as Wayne, even during the period when he first came to stardom as a transvestite rock star enjoying the patronage of David

Bowie during the early part of the 1970s, the end of the same decade saw the blossoming of Jayne as a low rent Marlene Dietrich (no offence intended to either lady). The quotation about whether the removal of Wayne's pain has affected his music as Jayne is difficult to answer, as her recorded output in the altered format is strictly limited numerically (only one LP) and apparently artistically (one reviewer described Jayne as: "Challenging every rock convention in the book, from vocal competence to gender roles to sound quality to the bounds of bad taste". Surely nothing can be that bad/good?).

Nevertheless, County's work as Wayne often plumbs depths previously undreamt of – his first semi-legendary epic was titled *Rock 'n' Roll Enema,* but perhaps the nadir of his career was an EP titled *Blatantly Offensive*, which included at least three tracks guaranteed to upset even the strongest stomach. Without much doubt, the best/worst of the three is *Toilet Love* (sample lyric "I love it when you smell my dirty socks" – fancy some more? OK, try this little triplet. "I love it when you make it with a bathroom plunger, When I make it with you it gives me a rush, You stick your head in the toilet and I give it a flush"). Marginally less offensive is Wayne's most notorious song, *If You Don't Want To Fuck Me, Fuck Off* (far more immediately obvious, but delivering its entire message in the title, which hardly qualifies as subtle on any account at all), while *Mean Motherfuckin' Ma* makes it an unsavory hat-trick. It is perfectly clear that Wayne will never get to Heaven, but there seems to be some doubt as to whether the other place will admit such an obviously demented person, either as Wayne or Jayne. Be gone – and never darken my hi-fi again!

Wayne County (c. Jill Furmanovsky)

B. A. Robertson

Sometimes,
the terrible ambition

to achieve the status of a rock star takes many years — there's no way that 90% of those who become stars eventually would disagree with even such a bold assertion. But sometimes, one man's machinations in that elusive quest for fame subsequently come to light, and make fascinating reading.

Such a man is B.A. Robertson (the latest in a series of variations around a relatively average name, presumably the one given to him by his parents). The first outbreak in the search for stardom by this individual came during the early 1970s, when he recorded an album titled *Wringing Applause* for the American Ardent label, under the name of Brian Alexander Robertson (although it must be clearly understood that there may exist an almost legion number of previous attempts at cracking the commercial kernel, which have so far not come to light — Robertson, to his credit, made no attempt to disguise this total failure of the LP already mentioned. In his introductory press release for his next solo LP (more of which in a moment), Robertson claimed that Ardent Records went out of business soon after he had finished the album, and that the LP was never issued. There may be some doubt as to the absolute accuracy of these assertions (— a copy of the LP sleeve should be pictured hereabouts. . .) An additional piece of information concerning this 'never released' LP was that it was produced by another fairly famous musician who apparently had an identity crisis — at the end of the 1960s, a folk/rock group called Eclection released a very creditable LP on Elektra Records, and a member of the group was one Georg Hultgrenm. By the time he came to produce *Wringing Applause* for Robertson, he had become Georg Kajanus, a name which he later used as the leading light of Sailor, a band who scored several hits during th mid-'70s.

At the beginning of 1975, Robertson seems to have been heading an organization known as Daniel Danzak and the Flying Scotsmen, who put together a 'group' which they called Apple Pie and Custard. It would be best to allow a reporter for the *Sunday Mail* of December 8, 1974, to continue the story:— "Apple Pie and Custard consist of four girls and five blokes and the oddest things about them is their garb. One dresses as a mechanic in overalls and has two large cardboard spanners tucked in his pockets. Another dresses as a military drummer. One is a sailor with red blobs on his cheeks and mouth — hello sailor — and another bloke wears a lop-sided green wig and lipstick. The girls — and some of the boys — wear stick out dresses, Mickey Mouse boots and wigs."

The group's single, *Five Sisters*, curiously failed to

be nominated for a Grammy Award at the time — stranger still, it did not succeed in topping the charts. Perhaps this somewhat belated publicity will make *Five Sisters* into the collector's item it was always destined to become, for not only was B.A. Robertson involved, but also a highly respected session musician, Herbie Flowers, now a leading light in classical/rock band Sky.

By mid-1976, Robertson had re-emerged to make a second solo LP, *Shadow Of A Thin Man* for Arista Records. This time he was well known as Alexander Robertson, and despite a massive (read 'overkill') publicity effort by the record company, this album again failed to dent (read 'approach by a thousand miles') the chart. But was he deterred by continual failure? Of course not — by 1979, he bounced back again, this time known as B.A. Robertson (another Brian Robertson, a substantially later arrival on the pop scene, as it's called in the business, had caught and passed the Brian Robertson we're studying here as one of the guitarists with heavy metal band Thin Lizzy).

Reverting to the Robertson saga, it was in 1979 that B.A. achieved his first hit, although even on this occasion, doubts were expressed as to whether success was truly deserved. The song in question was called *Bang Bang* (not the classic pop song recorded by such lovely ladies as Cher and Nancy Sinatra during the 1960s), and the somewhat dubious factor which tended to detract from the single's eventual position at number two in the chart was that the lyric contained a reference to the Managing Director of WEA Records at the time, John Fruin. It would be most incorrect to assume that John Fruin himself applied pressure to his staff to ensure that the record was a big hit — anyone who has met the man would find such an allegation difficult to believe — but during 1980, an

investigation by a television program took place into what was called 'chart hyping' — achieved by offering incentives to record shops to report sales of records in such a way as to improve their chances of initially appearing in the chart. After that, of course, increased radio exposure, the appearance of the record on chart listings and all the other supposedly automatic events which occur with a new chart entry, will occur, and if you're fortunate, like Mr. Robertson, you'll not only achieve a top three single, but also be able to follow it with some kind of repeat performance — B.A.'s subsequent single, *Knocked It Off* also made the top ten in 1979. Of course, since that time, John Fruin has resigned from WEA in the wake of (although not necessarily connected with) the chart hyping scandal — his replacement is another extremely pleasant gentleman named Charles Levison — to mention him in some future set of lyrics might be a bit heavy, son. . . But, joking apart, in terms of persistence, Brian Alexander, or Alexander, or B.A. ranks in the persistence league with one of the lady members of 1981 Eurovision Song Contest winners, Bucks Fizz, who cheerfully admitted that she'd been in two Eurovision groups before, and that every year, she submitted at least a dozen songs she'd written herself in the hope of gaining that vital break which comes with a Eurovision appearance. More power to them both!

The origins of the names of well known

recording acts sometimes conceal somewhat more dubious motives than are immediately obvious. One of the most popular bands to emerge during the British ska revival of 1980 was the multi-colored UB40. Unfortunately, a great many people may know exactly what a UB40 is when it doesn't refer to a group — it's the number printed on the Unemployment Benefit Attendance Card. Those who are unemployed through no fault of their own may question whether calling a band after this symbol of misfortune is in especially good taste, particularly as there is a strongly held theory that musicians in general are among the greatest abusers of the unemployment benefit system.

It may come as much more of a surprise to learn what was the original inspiration behind the name of the world famous 10cc — according to medical textbooks, this is the average amount of the male ejaculation, although why that should make it an attractive name for a band is something which is shrouded in mystery. Equally incomprehensible must be the fact that two of the four original members of

PRESUMABLY IN ORDER THAT EVERY lady newscaster shall have an equal crack of the whip in the wake of Wavis O'Shave's Love for Anna Ford (see elsewhere), a group has been formed with the unlikely name of Angela Rippon's Bum. As yet, neither the anonymous bum nor Ms. Rippon have felt moved to comment. . .

Frank Zappa and the Mothers of Invention

10.CC

UB40

10cc, Lol Creme and Kevin Godley, previously recorded under the name Frabjoy and Runcible Spoon. .

Yet another of the ska revival bands of 1980 also boasted a somewhat suspect appellation – Dexy's Midnight Runners. Dexedrine is the brand name of a very popular stimulant, the use of which precludes the need for sleep, and is therefore a prerequisite for those who indulge in the seemingly strange pastime of after hours athletics. Curiously enough, the name of Frank Zappa's famous band, the Mothers of Invention (said to be the second half of a famous quotation, "Necessity is the mother of invention") was apparently not the product of Zappa's often fertile mind. He first formed a group called The Mothers in 1963, but this folded when Zappa and co-conspirator 'Motorhead' Sherwood were jailed for ten days after being involved in the making of an apparently pornographic tape (although it should be noted that it is widely believed that Zappa had been 'framed' by the local vice squad. If this is in fact true, Zappa had the last laugh, because his prison record made him ineligible for military service, and he was thus spared a vacation in Vietnam). On his release, Zappa joined a Los Angeles band called The Soul Giants, whom he later renamed The Mothers. The suffix "of Invention" was apparently added by Zappa's record company of the time, Verve, who were anxious to recoup their at the time above average recording costs, and presumably felt that to call the less than attractive bunch simply "The Mothers" was not about to enhance their chances of turning a buck.

Dexys Midnight Runners

The life of
Keith Moon, erstwhile

drummer with The Who, has been well documented – his excessive behavior was rarely designed to be harmful to anyone other than himself, though his habit of walking the streets in full Nazi regalia did not help to lower the blood pressures of those around him. There were plenty of times when those unfortunate enough to get in the way of some of his more explosive antics must have wished that they had chosen that particular day to catch bubonic plague. Rolls Royces seemed to have great trouble keeping out of swimming pools when Keith was around. Moon's greatest problem was consuming boredom. As he told one reporter. "I took my axe and chopped the hotel room to pieces. The chairs, the television, the bed, all the furniture. It happens all the time."

He wasn't exaggerating, as his Who colleague Pete Townsend testified in an interview before Moon's death.

It happens with alarming regularity. Keith feels that he has to be involved in some form of entertainment all the time, even when the rest of the group may be asleep. He feels he has to entertain us and wake us, either by causing explosions or by getting us thrown out of the hotel. The first really big thing he did was on our first American tour, when he happened to go to Georgia, which was the only place in the States where you could buy fireworks, and they sell these things called cherry bombs. A few days later, I was in his room and all the paint around the door knocker was black where he'd been putting these things in the keyhole. I happened to ask if I could use his toilet, and he just smiled strangely and said I could. So I went in the bathroom, and there was no toilet – just a sort of S bend coming up out of the floor. I asked him what had happened, and he said that this cherry bomb had been about to go off in his hand, so he threw it into the toilet to put it out. I was surprised that they were powerful enough to destroy the toilet so utterly, and asked him, with fear in my eyes, how many he'd got. He said 'five hundred', opening up a suitcase which was full to the top with these things.

From that moment on, we were thrown out of every hotel we stayed in. The Holiday Inns were phoning round saying 'Don't let this group stay, because they'll blow the place up', and it got to the point where they were asking for five thousand dollars deposit to let us stay in even the shoddiest hotel. My nerves finally broke in New York. My wife was there, and we'd finally got to sleep when we were awoken by the sound of police cars outside. I went outside the room, and then I heard this great explosion which rocked the elevator. It transpired that he'd chosen to create an explosion in the hotel manager's wife's room, and so, of course, we got thrown out of that and every other hotel in New York, and for a long time afterwards, we had great difficulty in finding anywhere to stay in that city.

Later, he had this thing where he'd say things like 'Greatest hotel room I've ever seen – it was a work of art', and when you look in the room, it's total chaos, but he arranged it artistically – you didn't hear any great smashing noises, but when

Keith Moon

you looked in the room, it looked dreadful, although he hadn't actually broken anything, he'd just made it appear wrecked. He unscrewed cabinets and prised them apart, took the television out of its cabinet, stuck black sticky tape over the screen to make it look shattered, poured tomato ketchup in the bath and put a plastic leg sticking out of it. When we played towns in England, Keith would always find the joke shop – tear gas pellets and smoke bombs, stink bombs and itching powder in the bed, bugs under the pillow, naughty doggie in the sink.

Things have got a lot quieter since Moon's passing, and while The Who must in some ways be very glad that their days of being 'entertained' are over, perhaps they also sometimes miss the pranks of their famous drummer. . .

Few people would consider it an

advantage to pursue a career as a rock musician if one were unfortunate enough to be missing a limb. Obviously, certain limbs are more crucial than others to musicians of various types — it would hardly be a disadvantage, for example, for a trombone player, or in fact almost any player of a

Sandy Nelson

wind instrument, to be without a leg, although the loss of a finger might be a far more serious handicap for, say, a saxophonist.

Similarly, it might be thought that a drummer would be considerably handicapped by the loss of one of his feet, but this in fact happened to one of the most well known drummers of the vintage rock 'n' roll era, Sandy Nelson, who reached the top ten on both sides of the Atlantic on two occasions, in 1959 with *Teen Beat* and in 1961 with *Let There Be Drums*. However, between the making of these two hits, Sandy was badly injured in a car crash, resulting in the amputation of his left foot. Quite how he was able to continue playing his chosen instrument is difficult to imagine, but continue he definitely did — *Let There Be Drums* (recorded shortly after the crash) became his biggest hit, while two more percussive performances, *Drums Are My Beat* and *Drummin' Up A Storm*, made the top forty during the succeeding six months. Whether or not the painful effort required to function as a drummer became too much to bear after this is not known — suffice it to say that since his final hits in 1962, little has been heard of Sandy Nelson.

A similar occurrence came to light in the 1970s, with the brief rise to prominence of an American quartet known as Mose Jones. That their brush with the big time was brief was primarily due to the fact that they were signed to a small record label, Sounds Of The South, whose major stars were the extremely popular Lynyrd Skynyrd — in fact, Mose Jones recorded for the label some months before Skynyrd, but were unable to create the kind of excitement which made the latter one of the biggest attractions in the world before their career was suddenly terminated when several members of the band were killed in a plane crash. But that's another story — with the utmost respect to the music made by Mose Jones, perhaps the most interesting thing about the band was that their bass player, Randy Lewis, had no right hand. The group's first LP sleeve showed three different photographs of the band, and on each occasion, the fact of the missing limb is carefully (and to anyone who was unaware that Randy's hand is missing, imperceptibly) disguised. Al Kooper, who produced the group's first LP, was asked how Randy managed to play bass with such a handicap. "It's just too nauseating to describe", he said. However, the courage of a man with such a disability is undoubtedly to be admired, and it is sincerely to be hoped that if Randy is still involved in making music, that he enjoys all the luck in the world.

It should be emphasized at this point that the cases of Sandy Nelson and Randy Lewis are mentioned as tragic curiosities rather than reasons for derisory laughter. A final case is rather less clear cut — in 1965, a group from New England scored a reasonable hit with a song titled *Are You A Boy Or Are You A Girl*. A tongue in cheek opus about the social problems resulting from such groups as The Beatles and The Rolling Stones growing their hair long (and some may

find it interesting to note that certain parts of the United States have now turned full circle, and any male with short hair is the subject of often violent derision), the record has frankly failed to withstand the test of time, but The Barbarians have managed to outlive their brief musical fame to become a legend of sorts. This is entirely due to the fact that the group's drummer, who was known as Moulty, had a metal device instead of his left hand. In normal circumstances, he would appear to rank with Nelson and Lewis, but these two musicians took care never to draw attention to their handicap, while The Barbarians actually recorded a song titled *Moulty*, which consisted of the said individual delivering a soliloquy about his fight against his disadvantage. Whether this was a cunning ruse devised by the group or those around them to evoke sympathy and therefore huge record sales is not clear, but whatever the motive, the record is undeniably a kitsch classic, as Moulty explains, backed by a mournful harmonica, that something inside him urged him to battle against his misfortunes. Finally, he discovers that he loves music "and if you can make it at something you love, you've got it all", and the record ends with a plea — "Now there's one thing I need. Not sympathy, and I don't want no pity, but a girl, a real girl, one who really loves me". Taken at face value, there is some possibility that the sentiments expressed might be genuine, of course, in which case apologies are offered to the unfortunate Moulty and his colleagues. But if they're not. . .

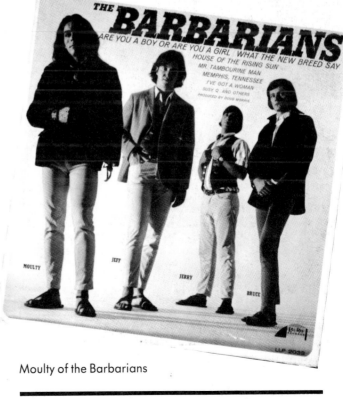

Moulty of the Barbarians

P. J. Proby

One of the earliest (and probably

saddest) victims of the pressures of success in the rock 'n' roll world was the semi-legendary P. J. Proby. Born James Marcus Smith in 1938, he allegedly first appeared on a local radio show at the age of eleven, and according to his own testimony, could also fly a full size helicopter at that age, although this boast seems a little on the unlikely side. When he was nineteen, James Marcus Smith renamed himself Jett Powers and moved to Hollywood, where he is supposed to have worked with the likes of Little Richard and B. B. King, although in what capacity is uncertain. He is also supposed to have formed a group with various others who later became Mothers of Invention, but again this is difficult to verify as more than rumor.

What has been better authenticated is that as Jett Powers, Proby was signed to Liberty Records as a songwriter and later as a performer, writing hits like *Clown Shoes* for Johnny Burnette and *Ain't Gonna Kiss Ya* for The Searchers, as well as making demonstration records of songs which other writers were trying to convince Elvis Presley to record — Proby was able to imitate Presley's style better than most. This relatively comfortable lifestyle continued until 1963, by which time Jett Powers/James Marcus Smith had become acquainted with Jack Good, the English television producer who almost single-handedly provided Britain, and later America, with a tradition of televised popular music whose influence remains today, with shows like *Six Five Special, Oh Boy* and *Shindig*. In 1964, Good was working on a TV spectacular titled *Meet the Beatles*, and invited our subject to England to be a special guest in the show, which was where the name P. J. Proby first surfaced.

An immediate success in the Beatles show, Proby started a run of Top Ten hits in Britain through 1964, including *Hold Me, Together* and an alarming version of *Somewhere*, which had previously been featured, although sung in a rather more sedate fasion, in *West Side Story*. By the end of 1964, Britain was at Proby's fingertips, and during January 1965, he began a nationwide tour which was to prove his undoing. During a concert at Croydon, Proby's trousers were so tight they split, which caused a minor sensation, but when the same thing occurred two days later during a Luton concert, it began to look less like an unfortunate accident and much more like a planned outrage. By the end of February, Proby was banned by most television companies in Britain and by several local councils in whose halls he was due to appear. Despite this furore, his records continued to sell, albeit often in lesser quantities, and he made the Top Fifty seven more times during 1965 and 1966, and even returned to America to make a film with his friend Bongo Wolfe, President of the American Count Dracula Society, called *Bongo Wolfe's Revenge*. This kept him fairly quiet during 1967, but by 1968, he had returned to Britain and released what turned out to be his final (minor) hit single, *It's Your Day Today*. Within a month, he had filed for bankruptcy, admitting assets of £10 and liabilities of £84,000. Various attempts at a comeback over subsequent years failed, perhaps the best chance being with an album titled *Three Week Hero* on which Proby was backed by the then newly formed Led Zeppelin, among other notable musicians. The title song may or may not have been written specially for Proby, but in later years, he may have been able to recognize the irony of the words of the song:

I'm a three week hero, I started out with zero,
And I sold a million records on my own.
Three short weeks ago, I was the lowest of the low,
I knew nothing — now there's nothing I don't know.

Those lines formed the chorus, and the final verse, with a little poetic license, documents the decline:

Now I'm no longer mobbed because my last two records bombed
And I squandered all the money that I had.
Now the guy that parked my car is a big recording star,
And all my friends are living at his pad.

As recently as 1978, Proby was given another opportunity to revive his flagging fortunes when fairy godfather Jack Good cast him as one of three different Elvis Presleys in the highly successful stage show *Elvis*. Unfortunately, by this time Proby had become rather unreliable, and he was fired from the show after a disagreement with the show's producers. Since then, the only sightings of P. J. have been in court; he was reported to be working as a porter in an apartment block, a very sad end for an undoubtedly gifted artist. His story is a very typical episode of life in the rock 'n' roll jungle but P. J. Proby must rank as one of the most talented and once-successful three week heroes around.

50
UNPLEASANT SONG TITLES

Dead Puppies   Ogden Edsel

Me and My Vibrator   Suzie Seacell

Walk On The Kosher Side
Gefilte Joe and the Fish

I Wanna Eat Your Pudding   Alvis Wayne

Boogie Woogie Amputee   Barnes and Barnes

Party In My Pants   Barnes and Barnes

Cemetery Girls   Barnes and Barnes

Being Boiled   The Human League

Armpit No. 6   Screaming Jay Hawkins

I'm Gonna Rough My Girlfriend's Boyfriend Up
Tonight   Guns For Hire

Go Funk Yourself   Juanita Goochifrita

Handles On Her Hips   Gillan

Love Like Anthrax   Gang Of Four

Dance For A Drop Of Blood   The Lines

Michael Booth's Talking Bum
Splodgenessabounds

You Can't Say Crap On The Radio
Stiff Little Fingers

99% Is Shit   Cash Pussies

Sympathy For The Devil   Rolling Stones

Kitten Kicker   Eugene and the Syncopators

Twat   John Cooper Clarke

I&f Boys Got Pregnant   The Orchids

Dare To Be Fat
Root Boy Slim and the Sex Change Band

The Gospel According to Rasputin   Slade

Sing If You're Glad To Be Gay   Tom Robinson

Belsen Was A Gas   Sex Pistols

Dead Pop Stars   Altered Images

Jerk Off All Night Long   Fred Banana

You Should See What I Do To You In My Dreams
Amber Squad

Per (version)   Mark Beer

Bite Me, I Taste Nice   Pete Bite

Sticky Death   Idol Death

Rabies   Naked Lunch

Bullshit Detector   Crass

Never Turn Your Back On A Liberal
Avant Gardeners

Dead Babies   Alice Cooper

Pretty Paedophiles   Raped

The Winker's Song (Misprint)
Ivor Biggun

Horrible Breath   Radio Stars

Loving A Killer   The Stoat

Orgasm Addict   Buzzcocks

Tell Me If You Wanna Bleed
Straight Eight

Nymphomania   Vermilion

Cure For Cancer   The Mirrors

Rock 'n' Roll Discharge
Deep Throat

For The Boys On The Dole
Neville Wanker and the Punters

Test Tube Babies   The Skids

The Murder of Liddle Towers
Angelic Upstarts

Psycho Mafia   The Fall

Farting with the Famous
Jackie Lynton's H. D. Band

Hungry Men No Longer Steal Sheep
But Are They Hanging Judges?   The Dole

Suck   Drac Rotten and the Vampires

SINGULARLY PAINFUL – singles and EPs

Death records – records concerning the

termination of a love affair due to one or both the parties dying – are in sufficient proliferation to become the subject of an entire book. This is not the place to list every death record made (a desperately depressing prospect, as anyone attempting the task would soon discover), but a few of the choicer items deserve a little illumination. Some of these, by the way, are funny, some are sick – it is a very personal matter to decide which is which . . .

One track which more often than not produced a guffaw is *Little Dead Surfer Girl* by the Incredible Broadside Brass Bed Band, taken from an album titled (for no good reason) *The Great Grizzly Bear Hunt* and released in America on the Poison Ring label. Played in a typical surf music style, it tells the story of how the singer and his girlfriend Rhonda go to the beach and attempt to surf, going out some distance, before it transpires that Rhonda is unable to swim. She therefore sinks, and as the singer remarks, "I'll never forget her last words to me – gurgle, gurgle, gurgle. Every night," he continues, "I go down to the beach, because I know that when the tide comes in, so does Rhonda." Of course, these things are all a matter of perspective – I suppose to anyone who has nearly drowned or who has lost a loved one in this way, this littel number from the IBBBB doesn't seem quite as laughable as it does to the rest of us.

The same must go for a track recorded by a very well known surf music act (a coincidence in fact, as the particular song under scrutiny is not a surf song at all). It's called *A Beginning From An End*, and mercifully briefly the story is that of a husband whose wife dies in childbirth. However, the child survives, and looks exactly like her late mother – "You never knew her, sweetheart, but she must have known you somewhere, because she looks, acts and talks the way I remember you." To be honest, this concept is pretty sick, as anyone involved in a similar occurrence would be upset to confirm. A lot of people have made one death record, but brand leaders in the field must be the Shangri-Las, the New York trio or sometimes quartet, who made at least four death tracks. The best known pair are the atmospheric *Leader Of The Pack*, where the boyfriend "roared into the night, accelerated his motorbike", and was then involved in a crash of terrifying proportions which is graphically illustrated on the record. The cut has become a bit of a classic and from the point of view of taste, no doubt many would feel that leaders of the pack deserve all they get. . .

I Can Never Go Home Anymore is a much more touching mini-epic, concerning a girl's advice to another who is about to leave home. The first girl recounts how she quarrels with her mother about the inevitable boy friend, eventually leaves home, but "can never go home any more" because she has broken her mother's heart, and "the angels have taken her to be their friend". Mawkish, perhaps, but effective in its way. But the crowning masterpiece by the Shangri-Las, written like *Leader Of The Pack*, by the highly successful songwriting team of Jeff Barry and Ellie Greenwich, and produced by the fractured genius of the remarkable George 'Shadow' Morton, is *Give Us Your Blessings*, whose storyline runs like this: Mary and Jimmy fall in love, and ask for their parents to approve of their impending wedding. The parents laugh at them, calling them children, so Mary and Jimmy decide to elope during a thunderstorm. They have, we are told, tears in their eyes, which is perhaps why Jimmy fails to see a sign on the road which reads 'Detour', and they plunge to their deaths.

TEEN ANGUISH VOLUME TWO

The Shangri-Las

THEIR GREATEST HITS

(courtesy Charly Records)

A particularly unhappy ending, but a record, like most of those by the Shangri-Las/Morton team, which is difficult to forget, especially as it deals with a fairly common adolescent problem – when even a death record deals with a topic with which many people can identify, it becomes much more easily assimilable.

Unlike the final grisly epic which should be mentioned in this section, a horrific, but really rather laughable song called *I Want My Baby Back* by someone called Jimmy Cross, whose grasp of the kitsch ethic is stronger than almost anyone in recorded history. This track achieved considerable infamy when it was selected as the lead track on an album called *The World's Worst Record Show*. We shall be returning to this album elsewhere in this book, but this track tells of a car accident, which leaves Cross' 'baby' in several pieces scattered over the road. So determined is Cross to "get his baby back" that he climbs into her coffin, having dug it up in the graveyard, and sings the final chorus of the song from inside her coffin. This offering plumbs the depths of unpleasantness although it may be argued by necrophiles that it is the most emotive record ever made.

WITHOUT ANY DOUBT WHATSOEVER, *one of the worst singles ever released was an attempt by Mrs. Elva Miller, a middle aged housewife who, like Florence Foster Jenkins, the opera 'chanteuse', believed that her voice was perfect for making records, but that some obscure grudge was held against her which prevented a record company from signing her up. As a result, she financed several recordings herself, which became kitsch classics of semi-classical music. Mr. Miller's case was a little different – she also believed that her voice was exceptional (although in reality, it was exceptional for totally opposite reasons to those which she believed), and an executive with a sense of humor at Capital Records in Hollywood signed her up. Her version of A Lover's Concerto, a 1965 hit for American female trio, The Toys, is perfectly excruciating, creating the curious effect of someone suffering hysterics while gargling with gasoline. Mrs. Miller induced mass migraine in the public with a number of other records before she fortunately lapsed into obscurity, from which, it is to be hoped, she will never re-emerge.*

The record which first brought

Lou Reed fame as a solo artist, *Walk On The Wild Side*, was a hit single which came from an album titled *Transformer* produced by David Bowie. Somewhat surprisingly, this single received considerable airplay in view of its lyrics, which were frequently fairly explicit, although couched in 'hip' terminology which might have been alien to radio programmers. The first two verses of the song (a kind of 'memorial' to some of the stars 'discovered' by Andy Warhol) were the ones with dubious contents:

Holly came from Miami, FLA,
Hitch-hiked her way across the USA,
Plucked her eyebrows on the way,
Shaved her legs and then he was a she...
'Candy came from out on the island,
In the backroom she was everybody's darlin'.
But she never lost her head,
Even when she was givin' head...

Transvestites and oral sex — definitely not an obvious diet for a family audience . . . but nevertheless, a fine record. Two other singles deserve mention in the oral sex stakes: Jefferson Starship's *Miracles* for the cute "I got a taste of the real world when I went down on you girl," and Blondie's "I'll give you some head — and shoulders to cry on."

ou Reed

SINGULARLY PAINFUL

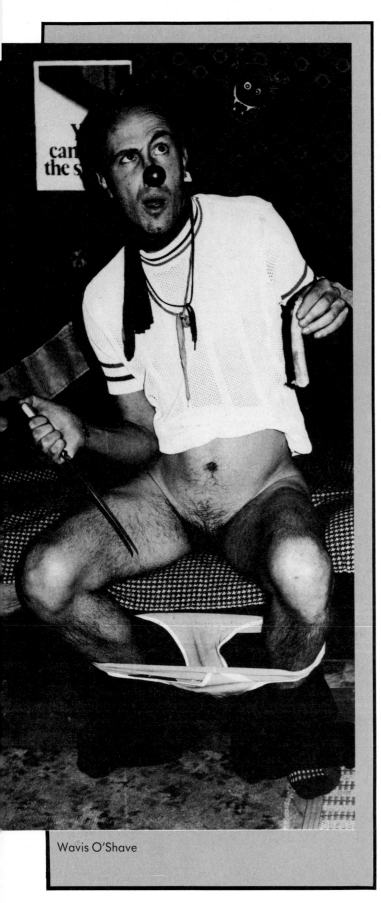

Wavis O'Shave

Among certain would be rock stars

there seems to be a feeling that to have any kind of musical talent is of comparatively minor importance — being noticed is what makes the difference between fame and obscurity. Of course, there are various ways in which this can be achieved, but one method which seems to have been in vogue since the late 1970s is to include the name of a famous person in your song title. In fact, it is very difficult to think of even one such act/song title which has achieved anything more than very insignificant minor notoriety for its perpetrator(s), and the vast majority of the attempts which are made are musically so ordinary and lyrically so insane that it is to be hoped that the practise soon disappears — the world is sufficiently short of oil as it is, without such a valuable commodity being wasted on meaningless ego-tripping attempts to jump on the gravy train to pop stardom.

One such effort which should have been forgotten, but which has somehow managed to rise to the surface, is a single by an individual from South Shields who calls himself Wavis O'Shave. Wavis told a weekly pop paper: "According to the dictionary, I'm mad. Crazy. I don't agree that there are taboos to be kept away from. You attain that state and it's wonderful. There's no restraint. It's great". The contribution to culture of this man who wears a three foot long false nose was a mini-LP (itself a fairly unconventional description) which Wavis titled *Anna Ford's Bum*, and he followed the escape of the disc with a proposal of marriage to the said lady. Although they have not so far made it to vinyl, a couple of other Wavis stratagems have included challenging the Pope to a boxing match (the winner to become the new Pope) and racing Jimmy Carter from the O'Shave residence to a local taxi rank and back for the Presidency (this was before the entire business of American politics itself deteriorated into farce).

Perhaps there's something about parts of Northern England that leads to desperate measures — a group from Market Drayton calling themselves The Notsensibles certainly did nothing perceptible to further the cause of anything at all when they recorded their most famous song, *I'm In Love With Margaret Thatcher*. This failed to create a media surge to Market Drayton to discover more about these emergent heroes, as did the other side of their single, which plumped instead for an attack via the media, in particular the weekly pop newspaper *Sounds*, one of whose writers, Garry Bushell, had gained a reputation for discovering a new band whom he considered "interesting" almost every week. However, calling this song *Garry Bushell's Band Of The Week* was just as doomed to failure as the Iron Lady epic. It is to be hoped that The Notsensibles will somehow be prevented from besmirching the names of either the Prime Minister or even Garry Bushell in future. . .

Wavis O'Shave with Anna Ford
(c.I.N. Competent)

In fact, all this seems comparatively tame next to what genuinely appears to be among the top ten most outrageous records of all time. Possibly the group involved were aware that nothing but notoriety could possibly result from their endeavors, which is why they called themselves The Rotters. And the title of their trasvesty? Well, it would perhaps be useful to understand that the lady upon whose good name (not to mention a certain other characteristic) the band were hoping to launch a career is an extremely attractive lady singer who has achieved international fame as a member of Fleetwood Mac. And the title of the record? I'm afraid it's called *Sit On My Face Stevie Nicks*. Is no-one safe from this kind of outrage?

Certainly not the most famous political family of the United States. A group from Berkeley California,

POSSIBLY THE MOST NEGATIVE SINGLE

ever to foist itself upon an undeserving public is Nobody But Me *by The Human Beinz which in just over two minutes manages the word* no *over 100 times and* nobody *46 times (they do throw in one* yeah *as a palliative), while the artist who has come closest to simulating the sensation for the listener of having a pick-up truck drive over his head is* Napoleon XIV *with his flip side of* They're Coming to Take Me Away, Ha-Haaa!, *which is namely* Aaah-Ah, Yawa Em Ekat Ot Gnimoc Er'yeht!

known as Little Roger and the Goosebumps, came up with something which, for a change, was actually quite listenable in musical terms (unlike the previous efforts in this category). Having flexed their muscles with a quite acceptable EP of songs by The Kinks, the group next turned their attention to Led Zeppelin, writing fresh lyrics to Zeppelin's classic *Stairway To Heaven* which linked the song with a popular U.S. television show, *Gilligan's Island*. This was prevented from gaining much exposure after Led Zep leader Jimmy Page heard the record and threatened a lawsuit. Thus far, Roger and the 'bumps hadn't really tried to use anyone else's name in their song titles, but during the summer of 1980, the group made one of the most interesting and acceptable (depending on your point of view) records of this type. Adapting Neil Young's classic *Cinammon Girl*, and slightly altering the lyrics from "I want to live with a cinammon girl, I could be happy the rest of my life with a cinammon girl" to "I want to live with a Kennedy girl, Plenty of money the rest of my life with a Kennedy girl", their song carried on 'Sister or cousin, it don't matter to me, On every branch of that family tree there are Kennedy girls'. On this occasion, no lawsuit appears to have been forthcoming, which would appear to mean, as was noted at the time, that Neil Young has a more keenly developed sense of humor than Jimmy Page. Whether or not this also applies to the famous Kennedy family is something which cannot currently be ascertained. . .

FEW WOULD DISAGREE THAT VIRGIN *Records, despite their often adventurous attitude towards the release of records which many would term controversial, occasionally suffer lapses of good taste, their appalling Sid Vicious posthumous LP being one example which readily comes to mind. It may be recalled that at one point, a single was released of British train robber Ronald Biggs singing with the Sex Pistols – during 1981, when a fresh furore over Biggs exploded concerning his possible deportation from exile in Brazil, Virgin took it upon themselves to release a single, supposedly "to focus attention on the current plight of Ronald Biggs, presently held in custody in Barbados." "The single,* Ronnie Biggs (He Was Only the Tea Boy)*", informed Virgin's press release, was recorded by members of the Great Train Robbery Gang, is their attempt to downplay Biggs' role as one of the principals in the crime, and certainly not one of the organizers, therefore hardly deserving his original thirty year prison sentence." It is pleasant to report that the single, whose proceeds, it was said, would be donated to those "looking after Ronald Biggs' son", vanished without trace within days of release. It is only such occurrences that allow those who have enjoyed popular music to retain even the smallest iota of faith in the medium. . .*

There is an element of greed

in the record industry which from time to time becomes less than amusing – amusement is the normal reaction to the news that someone who has little musical ability and no talent whatsoever as a singer has made a record, their only apparent advantage over ordinary mortals being that they are fairly famous in some totally different field of human endeavor. An unexpected invitation to make a record is a fairly accurate barometer of popularity, and while it may give the ego of the invitee a tremendous boost, it has very rarely, if ever, brought any joy to the staff and shareholders of the record companies who have been foolish enough to gamble on what must now be plainly seen as the kind of gamble where the house always wins.

There are numerous examples of this type of folly, and one day some advanced masochist who has tried ever other way he knows to torture himself may embark on this Holy Grail of Self-Abuse, searching our these records in the very appropriately named junk shops (probably the only place they are found more than two weeks after release). The examples which follow are, regrettably, merely the fruits of the memories of several people, as a comprehensive list of these less than classic items would only be prepared by an imbecile or the imaginary self abuser already imagined above.

During the 1970s, by far the most popular sporting pastime was soccer or Association Football, as it's called in Britain. There was something faintly heart-warming about the English 1970 World Cup Squad singing the patriotic *Back Home* as they departed for some foreign territory in a fruitless attempt to defend the trophy which they had won so convincingly at Wembley Stadium four years before, and in fact the record made by these mud-spattered magicians topped the charts for three terrible weeks during May 1970. Unfortunately, however, it was a signal for a rash of soccer-oriented singles to emerge. We should, of course, be eternally grateful that a lot of them failed to sell enough to enter the hit parade – otherwise, music as we know and sometimes love it stood a very fair chance of becoming a white elephant.

However, almost every year since 1970, there has been some kind of soccer record in the British charts, although fortunately, none has ever aspired to the chart topping heights of that first calamity. There was probably a good footballing reason why *Good Old Arsenal* by the players of said London club was appropriate in 1971, and perhaps the same goes for Leeds United's eponymous single and Chelsea F.C.'s *Blue Is The Colour* (this refers to their shirts, by the way, rather than the lyrics to their anthem) should sell well enough to make the top ten. 1973 saw a slight change in emphasis – a group of people who were supposedly ardent supporters of Tottenham Hotspur, a club whose emblem is a chicken dubbed themselves

The Cockerel Chorus and recorded a paean to one Cyril Knowles, the club's English international defender. The song was titled *Nice One Cyril*, a phrase which has since passed into the annals of everyday folklore. Whether or not any of those who sang on the record had ever watched Tottenham Hotspur play is unclear – what is certain, however, is that some of the 'singers' were actually employees of the various record companies who stood to gain some advantage if the record became a hit, which it did. More than one well known record industry face appeared in publicity pictures and on television. . .

1974 was the year of the World Cup again, and on this occasion, England failed to qualify for the Finals, the only representative of the British Isles being Scotland. With a dash of the typical subtlety which has made Scottish soccer supporters feared throughout

> **THE SONG MRS BROWN YOU'VE GOT** a Lovely Daughter *is fairly well known (it was a 1965 million seller for Herman's Hermits), but how many have heard the 'sequel', a charming little ditty apparently using a similar tune, and performed by Kenny and the English Muffins, titled* Mrs. Green You've Got An Ugly Daughter. *Very colorful . . .*

the world (and that is no exaggeration), the Scottish squad recorded *Easy Easy*, which just made the top twenty, while the football team did little better. There seemed to be a chance of the whole dreadful epidemic coming to a merciful end when the next year, 1975, saw no soccer hit, of any sort, but

Liverpool F.C.

SINGULARLY PAINFUL

unfortunately, the following year's chart was dented, albeit only for one week, by an eponymous anthem created by Manchester United. '77 was a big year for Liverpool, sufficiently significant for them to release a single with four tracks on it of varying relevance to their team, and this put the game briefly back in the top twenty, a position which Nottingham Forest, although hugely successful on the field during 1978, were unable to equal when they recorded *We've Got The Whole World In Our Hands* that year, even despite some musical assistance from a well known local group called Paper Lace (who themselves had topped the charts in 1974 with the mawkish *Billy Don't Be A Hero*.

1979 saw a further change of emphasis – teams, apparently, were out of favor as far as record companies went. It was individuals who smelt of filthy lucre this year, a point underlined when Arsenal reached the F.A. Cup Final and released a single titled *Super Arsenal F.C.*, which signally failed to impress the record buying public. It would perhaps by appropriate to quote a portion of the lyrics in order that the reader can judge whether or not this rejection was justified. . .

With the big man behind you you're safe at the back,
And Sammy and Pat move it into attack,
There's David O'Leary and big Willie Young,
Sending Rixie and Stapleton off on a run.

You can almost hear Sir John Betjeman, the Poet Laureate, preparing to emigrate in the certain knowledge that his writing would never be compared with such wit, fluency and command of the English language.

To return to the point, the only soccer hit of 1979 was *Head Over Heels In Love* by England captain Kevin Keegan, who had formed some kind of mutual admiration society with Bradford quartet Smokie, makers of numerous hits on their own account. This led to the group assisting Keegan with his record which, although it seemed not to mention the subject of soccer, was generally regarded as unbelievably bland. Still, it wasn't much like the archetypal soccer record, featuring a dozen or more untrained voices shouting around an appallingly trite tune lyrics of a similar quality, for which I suppose, the world should have been grateful.

The next step was a genuine group apparently composed of soccer supporters. Some may take exception to the world 'genuine' – one reviewer called a single by the band in question, The Cockney Rejects, "a horrible harangue," and that was one of the more polite write-ups – but certainly, the record was made by three people with instruments backing the somewhat manic shouts of vocalist Stinky Turner, and the song they chose to mutate was *I'm Forever Blowing Bubbles*, which had been adopted as the theme tune of the fans of West Ham United, who had reached the

ONE OF THE MORE UNLIKELY

recording acts to have appeared during the 1970s was someone called The Legendary Lonnie, although his actual existence may only be a figment of the imagination of his publicist, as the following excerpts from his 'biography' seem to illustrate: By fourteen, he was playing the guitar and singing outside his local Odeon cinema, prior to joining a local skiffle group called Caca Brown and the Blowoffs – later renamed Dysentery. He became noted for his bizarre stage clothes, which usually consisted of a policeman's helmet, building site donkey jacket, knee-length Stanley Matthews-style soccer shorts, McAlpine rubber boots and, naturally, his self-designed guitar shaped like a garden shovel. He began recording about 1956 with No Chance Records, and later with Flakeout, Loser, Ripoff and Deadbeat. He began recording for Bottoms Up in May 1958. They issued Constipation Shake, which turned out to be a real bummer and bombed out. It sold exactly four copies and became the New York label's worst selling single, forcing Lonnie into temporary recording retirement. During the next ten years, Lonnie had a number of jobs, including barman, poultry trusser, undertaker, sponge diver and dolphin trainer. He also found the time to record as a New Wave artist under the name Nose Mucus and the Bogeys, and added a punk rock record entitled Vomit On Me to his credit. Lonnie is one of the most powerful songwriters in the music business, having an 18" neck, 19" biceps, a 52" chest and the kind of varicose veins that look like a map of Scotland." Anyone but the most inexperienced hack would immediately recognize the work of Britain's most verbally inventive publicist especially when it comes to an act whose music is vintage rock 'n' roll music (as The Legendary Lonnie was made out to be). The sad truth, however, is that The Legendary gent possibly sold even fewer than the four copies of Constipation Shake mentioned in the biography of the single being hustled, which was, in case anyone may be interested, titled Wine Glass Rock, "an instrumental that Legendary Lonnie plays with the drinking edge of a wine glass". And if you believe that. . .

F.A. Cup Final, a significant feat for a team from the Second Division of the English Football League. The Rejects pursued the soccer record concept, recording tracks like *War On The Terraces*, but following charges against the group's guitarist, Micky Geggus, which meant that he faced possible life imprisonment if found guilty, they have been somewhat quieter of late.

By now, of course, several permutations of soccer records had been attempted with extremely varied degrees of success (it should be noted that the discs so far mentioned are almost literally the cream of the

ANOTHER AMBITIOUS ATTEMPT

(although reportedly not in musical terms) to gain fame by proxy was the release by a group named International Pen Pals of a single titled The Story Of The Day They Ate Ronald Reagan. Turning the disc over, one found a series of extracts from Richard Nixon's speech of resignation. All president and incorrect?

crop), and the start of the 1980/1 tottball season saw more new ideas. One combined the musical possibilities presented by making a single with England's two foremost goalkeepers, Peter Shilton of Nottingham Forest and Ray Clemence of Liverpool, who are invariably described in tabloid newspapers as "friendly rivals". The song which they recorded was, of course, *Side By Side*, but despite the seeming ingenuity of appealing to the supporters of two famous clubs and the national team, the record was not a major success. Neither was another innovation, a record made by a football manager, Brian Clough of Nottingham Forest, who was cajoled into recording something called *You Can't Win 'Em All* as a kind of duet with J. J. Barrie, an Australian opportunist with an American accent — Barrie sings a chorus of a sub-Eurovision song which, according to the credits, took three people to compose — very surprising, that, if you ever hear it — after which Brian comes in with a monolog beginning "Hi, it's Clough here", and continuing with twenty seconds of platitudes before Barrie returns with a couple more choruses, followed by a commentary on some soccer game which may or may not be relevant to Brian Clough and/or the team he manages. Clough is heard again for another ten seconds, urging supporters not to take out their team's failure to win matches on innocent bystanders etc., and isn't heard from again. The record lasts for around three and a half minutes, of which Clough is in evidence for little more than thirty seconds. The other side of the record purports to feature Clough again, this time with his assistant, Peter Taylor, with a song titled *It's Only A Game*. Once more, Clough's contributions are severely limited. What is perhaps most surprising about this record is that such an obviously intelligent, self-opinionated, man as Brian Clough should allow himself to be inveigled into what can only be seen as a cheap gimmicky attempt to worm money out of the pockets of soccer supporters who can possibly ill afford to spend it in exchange for a record which any self-respecting intelligent person would not allow in his home. I wonder how Clough would feel if Elton John, himself a ardent football supporter and chairman of Watford F.C., were to use his position of authority and insist on being selected for the club's first team?

Everything else pales into insignificance

beside a three track Australian single released (or should that be 'unleashed'?) by an Australian label which calls itself *Numbat Adoration*, the significance of which seems to escape this writer. As well as a cover version (and this is redolent of the Rotters' swiftly banned love song to the lady in Fleetwood Mac, *Sit On My Face, Stevie Nicks*, one of the tracks is titled (on the record label) *Beep! — Me Forever*, written, we are informed, by Ms Connie Lingus. The lyrics to this epic dwarf in grossness anything else which appears in this volume, a sample being the following:

Fuck Me Forever, Let me forever come, come,
Fuck me forever, till I'm blind, deaf and dumb.
Make your sweet cock, Hard as a rock,
Oh fuck me forever, let this ecstasy never end,
I can't stand the pain, but please fuck me again.

If this were not gross enough, the 'song' is performed by a lady singer who could be quite easily mistaken for a country and western croonerette influenced by any one of a score of cowgirls from Nashville. It seems somehow doubtful that any cover versions of this particular song will come to light. The final track (what passes for the A side of the record) is titled *Stickball*, and is unbelievably unpleasant and it revolts your humble scribe so totally that no more will be said about it, other than that it involves blasphemy and a series of often unnatural acts, and that it is difficult to believe that anyone in their right mind could have come up with anything quite so crass. Undoubtedly, a classic, but as the perpetrators note on the label, "Public performance of these tracks is the very last thing you ought to do — honest!" It is minimally reassuring to note this small element of contrition . . . but at times like this, even ole M. Raker begins to debate whether writing this volume was such a good idea after all.

Do Fleetwood Mac know about this record?

Adrian Munsey and the Lost Sheep

Most eccentric

One of the most unlikely records ever released was by an act known as Adrian Munsey and the Lost Sheep, which the company who released it described as 'introducing a new category of popular music — middle of the field (MOF)'. Munsey, apparently, was a Departmental Head at the London College of Printing, among other things, and claimed to have recorded the sheep (who appear on the records making the only noise of which sheep are capable, i.e. baa-ing) in a small studio in Hendon, and the wind 'on location in Dorset'. The press release continues "200 orders for the record have been placed by the International Wool Secretariat to send to fashion journalists, and Munsey hopes that shepherds will buy it and play it to their sheep. There are thirty million sheep and nineteen million lambs in the UK. This record is about three of them". Someone with a highly developed sense of the ridiculous even arranged for Munsey, plus a sheep or two, to appear on a TV chat show, and as a result, he later released a follow up single, 'C'est Sheep', "as an assault on the disco field (get it, field)", which was produced by Ron and Russell Mael of Sparks. Like its predecessor, the second single effectively vanished without trace, and the wool was no longer pulled over the public's eyes. . .

A number of records came out

during the period when American hostages were imprisoned in Iran. Two in particular are worth mentioning here: to the tune/arrangement of *Barbara Ann* by both The Regents and The Beach Boys, Vince Vance and the Valiants perform *Bomb Iran*, sample lyrics reading as follows:

Went to a mosque, Gonna throw some rocks,
Tell the Ayatallah gonna put him in a box.

and

Old Uncle Sam's getting pretty hot,
Time to turn Iran into a parking lot.

That particular little piece of poetry was conceived apparently in Nashville, of all places, and came forth and multiplied on a label named Paid. On a similar theme, although from an unknown source, came a similarly slanted piece of invective on the hitherto unkown Renta-Hits label. This one, performed to the tune of *My Sharona*, a song which was one of the biggest American hits of all time, was titled *Ayatollah* and the artists concerned are credited as Steve Dahl and Teenage Radiation.

Barbara Ann was somewhat less than the most subtle song ever written, and even allowing for any shortcomings which might be found in *My Sharona*, the latter is an infinitely more intelligent song (although this is akin to comparing say, a ferret with a rabbit as a useful companion in the search for gold), a judgment which also applies to the lyrics of *Ayatollah*, which at times verge on being actually witty, as follows:

You've got a real nice beard, a real nice beard,
You know it really caught my eye, Atollah,
But your mind is weird, your mind is weird,
You really are a nutty kind of guy, Ayatollah.

When you get the Shah back, the Shah back home,
We know you're going to eat him on rye, Atollah.
But we kind of need your oil to make our gas,
You know you're such a pain in the eye, Atollah.
Don't get us too upset, or we'll do something
nuclear . . . Bye, Atollah. . .

Americans are mostly cool, mostly cool,
But now we're really starting to fry, Atollah,
And you know, if you were here, if you were here,
We'd hit you in the face with a pie, Atollah. . .

and so on. Perhaps the fact that songs like this seem only to appear in times of crisis indicates that at least some Americans tend to become more creative in adversity . . . And just to underline the joke, the record's catalog number is KOMEN I.

The lyrics which follow are those

to a single which made the American top ten during 1967. The voice which intones the lyrics to a backdrop of a choir singing *The Battle Hymn Of The Republic* ("Glory, glory hallelujah" etc.) is almost a cross between those of Lyndon Johnson and Richard Nixon (making sure that the appeal is to both sides of the political coin) and belongs to one Lunberg, the owner of an advertising firm in Grand Rapids, Michigan, who had served in the Psychological Warfare Department of the U.S. Army during the Second World War, and later worked as a local radio station announcer before founding his advertising agency. Possibly, this almost unique background explains why the record, a million seller, was constructed in the particular way in which it appeared.

Dear Son.
You ask my reaction to long hair or beards on young people. Some great men have worn long hair and beards. George Washington and Abraham Lincoln. If, to you, long hair and a beard is a symbol of independence, if you believe in your heart that the principles of this country, our heritage, is worthy of this display of pride that all men shall remain free, that free men at all times will not inflict their personal limitations or achievement on others, to demand your own rights as well as the rights of others, and be willing to fight for this right, you have my blessing.
You ask that I not judge you merely as a teenager, to judge you on your personal habits, abilities and goals. This is a fair request, and I promise I will not judge any person only as a teenager, if you will constantly remind yourself that some of my generation judges people by their race, their belief, or the color of their skin, and that this is no more right than saying all teenagers are drunken dope addicts or glue sniffers. If you will judge every human being on his own individual potential, I will do the same. You ask me if God is dead. This is a question each individual must answer within himself. Could a warm summer day with all its brightness, all its sound, all its exhilerating breathiness, just happen? God is love – remember that God is a guide, and not a storm trooper.
Realize that many of the past and present generation, because of a well intentioned, but unjustifiable misconception, have attempted to legislate morality. This created part of the basis for your generation's need to rebel against our society. With this knowledge, perhaps your children will never ask 'Is God dead?' I sometimes think much of mankind is trying to work him to death.
You ask my opinion of draft card burners. I would answer this way – all past wars have been

dirty, unfair, immoral, bloody and second guess. However, history has shown most of them necessary. If you doubt that our free enterprise system in the United States is worth protecting, if you doubt the principles upon which this country was founded, that we remain free to choose our religion, our individual endeavors, our method of government, if you doubt that each free individual in this great country should reap rewards commensurate only with his own efforts, then it's doubtful you belong here. If you doubt that people to govern us should be selected by their desire to allow us to strive for any goal we feel capable of attaining, then it's doubtful you should participate in their selection. If you are not grateful to a country that gave your father the opportunity to work for his family, to give you the things you've had, and you do not feel pride enough to fight for your right to continue in this manner, then I assume the blame for your failure to recognize the true value of our birthright. And I would remind you that your mother will love you no matter what you do, because she is a woman. And I love you too, son – but I also love our country, and the principles for which we stand. If you decide to burn your draft card, then burn your birth certificate at the same time. From that moment on – I have no son.

A few historical points emphasize the impact which this record had on American parents (although on a lesser percentage of their children). On August 31, 1965, it became illegal to burn draft cards, although this move was obviously most unpopular, and, possibly escalated their burning into an epidemic. Just over two months after the bill to make card burning illegal was passed through the Senate, one youth, a Quaker, burned himself to death in front of the Pentagon in protest, and by February 1966, draft card burning conventions were being held. Whether or not Victor Lunberg's obviously well meaning, but often unintentionally humorous, message was understood by those at whom it was aimed is difficult to say. However, the record's success was even stranger when it is taken into account that at the beginning of October 1967, statistics were published relating to the more than thirteen thousand dead and nearly one thousand missing American soldiers in the Vietnam war. Even so, the record achieved over one million sales within a month of release, and spawned an album along the same lines.

PERHAPS THE RECORD WHICH ENJOYED the most limited distribution was a single by the pseudo-comedy group, Brother Lees, which was released only in the seaside town of Cleethorpes in the North of England. The group (?) was apparently performing in a summer season at the town's Pavillion Pier, and in order, presumably, to satisfy some local demand, the single was made available only to local record shops, as well as being on sale in the theater foyer. The title of the record, by the way, was The Night The Orchestra Died, and due to the fact that the author has managed to avoid going to Cleethorpes, to comment on its quality, or lack of it, would hardly be appropriate. . .

The realms of vampire rock seem to

include very few items – the record which receives most attention is probably *Monster Mash* by Bobby 'Boris' Pickett and the Crypt-Kickers, which has been a hit in Britain more than once. However, the consensus of opinion among those who have ever managed to hear it, is that a much superior record is *Dinner With Drac* intoned by Philadelphia disc jockey/television personality John Zacherle, known during his heyday as the 'cool ghoul'.

Inevitably, the lyrics to this epic, despite being delivered in a Karloff-like voice, tended to be humorous, and are worth an extract:

Dinner was served for three, at Dracula's house by the sea.
The hors d'oeuvres tasted fine, but I choked on my wine,
When I learned that the main course was me.

The waitress, a vampire named Perkins, was so very fond of small gherkins,
That one day for tea, she ate forty three,
Which pickled her internal workings.

What a swimmer is Dracula's daughter, but the pool's a little more red that it oughta,
The blood stains the boat, but it's easy to float,
Because blood is much thicker than water.

For dessert, there was batwing confetti, and the veins of a mummy named Betty,
I first frowned upon it, but with ketchup on it,
It tasted very much like spaghetti.

This peculiar single actually reached number six in the American charts during 1958, seeming to indicate that Zacherle's sense of fun appealed to many other people, but somewhat curiously, the record thereafter fell into disrepute though it did find its way onto a late '70s compilation LP.

Fortunately, at least one rock 'n' roll scholar had not forgotten *Dinner With Drac*, which he decided to record himself, and release on his own Thrust label

Bobby 'Boris' Pickett

John Lewis Wagstaff was at the same time incensed by the publicity photograph of Kris Kristofferson and Barbara Streisand which accompanied their updated remake of the Judy Garland film, *A Star Is Born*, to the extent that he renamed himself Lee Kristofferson, for the purposes of his version of *Dinner With Drac*, and created a magnificent spoof of the utterly nauseating film photograph. Lee himself naturally played the Kristofferson role, while the Streisand part in the shot was taken by an anonymous lady. Aside from the different faces, the only other difference was that the lady had two drops of blood from puncture marks on her neck, making the new photograph particularly relevant to *Dinner With Drac*. Additionally, Wagstaff added a couple more verses, which are fairly amusing, although more in a limerick style than Zacherle's originals:

A cat in despondency sighed
And resolved to commit suicide
He ran under the wheels
Of eight automobiles
And under the ninth one he died.

There was a girl named Irene
Whose hair was a bright shade of green
When asked how she died it
She simply confided
I just use the juice from my spleen.

The world awaits with indifference Lee Kristofferson's follow up.

SELF-WORSHIP MADE SIMPLE – the ego page

Stars of popular music

are not, of course, well known for their reserve and modesty. A good example is that John Deutschendorff, better known to the world as John Denver. One of Denver's more memorable quotes is: "I can do anything. One of these days, I'll be so complete that I just won't be human anymore, I'll be a God". Denver is also a patriot, although another of his celebrated sayings, "I epitomize America", might easily lead you to believe otherwise . . . If Denver does in fact epitomize America, that country must lack the ability to laugh at itself, because when those well-known British humorists, the Monty Python team, included a brief track on their *Contractural Obligation* LP titled *Farewell To John Denver*, Denver immediately started legal proceedings to have the track removed from the record. In order that this bijou masterpiece's concept shall not be lost to posterity, it should be noted that an announcement is made that the next sound will be that of John Denver being strangled. After one line of music not dissimilar to his biggest British hit, *Annie's Song*, whoever is singing is indeed apparently strangled. Where, you may ask, is the harm in that? A God who epitomizes America would surely be omniscient enough to ignore such an obvious joke – at least they mentioned his name . . .

John Denver

It has been said

of Frank Sinatra (and although he'd probably vomit at the thought of being included in a book about rock 'n' roll, this quote might easily have been attributed to numerous rock 'n' rollers) that his idea of a perfect date with a girl is sitting in a darkened room listening to his own records.

Marc Bolan

Marc Bolan, as noted

elsewhere, was not considered an especially modest person, but perhaps the quote which best sums up his attitude to his own genius is this one: "If God came into my room, I'd obviously be awed, but I don't think I'd feel humble. I might cry, but I know he'd dig me like mad". If Marc made it up as opposed to down after his fatal acident, he'll presumably have discovered whether or not he was right. . .

One of the great

ego-trippers of the rock world must have been Walden Robert Casotto, professionally known as Bobby Darin. Darin's career was not without its hiccups, and before he achieved his breakthrough with *Splish Splash* in 1958, Darin was on the verge of being dropped by his record company due to his lack of success. Finally, of course, Darin made it, quickly establishing himself as a major star, but even his early struggles did not prevent him from telling one reporter: "I'm great; perhaps the best singer around these parts – these parts being the world." Darin was also proud of his manager. "He's a genius, you know. But I'm an even bigger genius for recognizing his potential". It may have been in the same interview when Darin modestly claimed: "I'll be a show business legend by the time I'm twenty five. Bigger than Sinatra? Certainly – I'll definitely be a legend". Darin certainly scored enough hit records in a comparatively short time to warrant consideration for the 'legendary' tag, but he unfortunately died at the age of thirty seven after open heart surgery: a legend purely in his own mind.

Bobby Darin

The Knack who

burst into the big time during 1979 with their hit single *My Sharona* and then forgot to stop, completing the big circle to return to anonymity, were highly thought of during their brief period of fame by groupies. Lead singer Doug Fieger noted: "Girls come to our shows because they want to go to bed with us without worrying that afterwards, we'll treat them like whores or sluts. They're pure, pretty, and incredibly horny". They probably have brains like rhinoceri. . .

The Knack

TORTURE AT 33¹₃ – albums

THERE ARE PLENTY OF BIZARRE incidents in which Lou Reed has been involved, not least a double LP which he released during the 1970s which he called Metal Machine Music. For once, no reviewer was able to find a kind word to say about this – one critic described it as: "a series of random electronic bleeps and squawks, with each side lasting exactly sixteen minutes and one second". This led to a rumor that while two of the record's four sides were actually recorded with some point in mind, the other two sides were actually the first two played backwards. Due to the fact that no-one will admit to having played right through Metal Machine Music (the usual excuse being that life is too short), the truth about this remains obscure – certainly, a fitting punishment for the most foul of crimes might be to play the album endlessly to a prisoner in a cell as after an hour or two, even the strongest willed person would be likely to be begging for mercy. . .

There will doubtless be attempts

to compile albums and/or tapes of choice cuts which are mentioned in this book, but the fact that many of these slabs of sleaze are owned by record companies who would probably not wish their products to be selected for collections of this type is one reason why such is unlikely to be released commercially. However, occasionally some near sighted genius gathers the courage to put together an album of this strange type of material, for better or worse. . .

One such is *The World's Worst Record Show* on the aptly titled Yuk Records, a twenty track catalog of mayhem collected after disc jockey Kenny Everett featured what he considered the most dreadful commercially released records on a London local radio station. We've already met Jimmy Cross and the ghoulish *I Want My Baby Back*, and several other death tracks are included, like the horrendous *The Deal* by Pat Campbell, which describes the dilemma of a husband who is told by a doctor that complications have arisen during the impending birth of his child, and that the husband will have to choose between saving either his wife or his as yet unborn

offspring. The husband is told he has little time and goes to the hospital chapel and makes the deal of the title with God: the basis of the agreement is that both mother and child will live, but the husband will go to meet his maker instead.

This is obviously not extraordinarily funny (something which could be said of all too many death discs), and the same goes for another track on this execrable LP, *Laurie* by Dickie Lee, which concerns the protagonist meeting a girl named Laurie at a dance, with whom he gets on very well. So well, in fact, that he walks her home, on the way lending her his sweater as she indicates that she feels cold. Having kissed Laurie goodnight, the boy begins to walk home himself, but remembering the sweater, returns to Laurie's house to retrieve his garment. A man answers the door, and is aghast at the request for the return of the sweater, telling the boy that his daughter Laurie actually died on her previous birthday. A subsequent visit to the local cemetery confirms this story, but there, on her grave, is the missing sweater. Sick? You betcha.

Still on the same side of the LP, at least one track can be found which is genuinely quite clever, if still a touch on the unpleasant side. The artist in this case is an erstwhile hitmaker of the 1950s who was born Jimmy Drake, but was professionally known as Nervous Norvous. Almost every record Drake made could be classed as a 'novelty' disc, although in 1956, he hit upon a purple patch which produced three American hit singles within six months. In Britain, the only one of the trio which made much impression at the time was a bizarre disc titled *Ape Call*, doubtless designed (and largely succeeding) as an impression of what a singing monkey might sound like. *Ape Call*, however, is not the track by Norvous which was chosen for *The World's Worst Record Show* – what was selected is a particular gruesome (but rather amusing) song titled *Transfusion*, wherein the singer recounts a catalog of motor accidents in which he has been involved. After each disaster, he apologizes to a medical attendant, before coming out with a sly rhyming couplet, like: 'Slip the blood to me, bud', 'Pour the crimson in me, Jimson', 'Pass the claret to me, Barrett' or 'Shoot the juice to me, Bruce'. This is a rather subtle song, in fact, and one whose nuances take several plays to fully comprehend. Then there's someone (or something) called The Legendary Stardust Cowboy, who commits unprecedented atrocities on a song titled *Paralysed*. From the songwriting credits, this appears to be a different song from that which Elvis Presley recorded in his earliest (and best) recording years — it is difficult to understand quite what LSC is singing about. More obvious rubbish comes in the shape of *Wunderbar*, as sung by Zarah Leander, *Spinning Wheel* by Mel and Dave, and a track from the only artist on the album represented by three tracks, Jess Conrad. Always more famous for his photogenic qualities than his very drab voice, the track by Conrad on side one is *This Pullover* — added to his lack of recognizable singing talent, the song must qualify as an all time low.

The same applies to the already mentioned final track on this side of the LP, *The Drunken Driver* by Ferlin Husky. Husky is quite well known as a Country & Western performer who achieved several conventional hit records, either under his own name, or that

Paul Anka

of a curious alter ego, Simon Crum. However, *The Drunken Driver* is a song (or rather a monolog) of such extraordinary grossness that almost anything pales beside it. In brief, the story is of two small children, whose mother has recently died, and whose father has deserted them. The children are walking along a road hand in hand when a drunken driver fails to miss them. The song describes in graphic detail how the car's bumper instantly kills the little girl and leaves the small boy lying in a ditch in a pool of blood, dying. The drunken driver gets out of his car to inspect the havoc he has wreaked, and recognizes the children as his own — he is the father who deserted the children, and he "prays for God to forgive him". The boy, with his dying breath, whispers "Daddy, why did you do that? We were talking about you and mommy, and I was telling little sister that we'd see you again some day. But why did it have to be this way?" The expression, I believe, is — follow that. . .

Inevitably, the second side of the record has a hard time following this catalog of calamities, although there are some truly terrible tracks typified by a 1956 monolog by British TV personality Eamonn Andrews who delivers a disastrous monolog entitled *The Shifting Whispering Sands*, which appears to concern someone lost in a desert and eventually dying there, although as it is the singer (Eamonn) who is lost, it is less than clear how it comes about that he can sing the song. It is a little unnerving to note that in 1956, this record reached the top twenty in Britain — thank goodness standards have raised themselves subsequently . . . not that the other two Jess Conrad tracks, which post-date Eamonn's travesty, are any improvement.

Why Am I Living? is the first of the two, and is simply pathetic, apart from any cheap directing of the question at the singer, while *Cherry Pie* is nothing more or less than a perfect example of a meaningless song performed by a vocalist with little discernible vocal ability. Similar remarks could be aimed at Steve Bent's *I'm Going To Spain*, a ballad about the singer going to Spain because his cousin had "a real fine time last year" and "it doesn't rain". Almost too inoffensive to warrant comment here, while another of the tracks on this side of the album is actually a punk rock classic, *Surfin' Bird* by the Trashmen. The vocal is certainly a little, er, unconventional, but this is a track with some rock 'n' roll credibility and hardly deserves its inclusion here.

Kick Out The Jams by Tub Thumper seems to be nothing more than a typical twelve bar surf instrumental with added sound effects of machine guns, sirens and a crowd seemingly recorded at one of Hitler's youth rallies. Again, too ordinary to really induce a cringe, and the same goes for *My Feet Start Tapping* by some one called Adolph Babel and an unidentified female — better to have included the genuinely awful *You're Having My Baby* by Paul Anka and Odia Coates, a single which was a huge worldwide hit as recently as 1974. Maybe that'll be on

John and Yoko Lennon

a second volume – and a simply bad version of *Goin' Out Of My Head* by some dago named Raphael, who sings half the song in heavily accented English and half in what is presumably his native tongue. Not really bad enough to warrant being on the record, but there can be no complaints about the inclusion of *The Big Architect*, yet another monolog, this time by erstwhile disc jockey Duncan Johnson, which is particularly offensive just because someone has tried so hard to prevent it being so. A glance at the title of *The Greatest Star Of All* might lead one to suppose that this was 'inspired' by the same subject, i.e. God, but you may be distressed to find that it in fact concerns Elvis Presley. The song is performed to a very fair country & western backing by someone named Skip Johnson, who sounds unnaturally like a younger version of Max Bygraves, which in itself may send many people screaming for the 'off' switch, but basically, the second side of *The World's Worst Record Show* comes as either a disappointment or a welcome relief, depending on your point of view. However, the tracks by Jimmy Cross, Pat Campbell, Dickie Lee and especially Ferlin Husky on side one make this a record either to cherish or destroy.

IN THE WAKE OF JOHN LENNON'S

murder, his widow Yoko Ono recorded and released her own LP, which she invited Phil Spector, who had previously worked with Lennon, to produce. Prior to this, Yoko's performances had often been criticized in the vein of "an animal being tortured" or "a noise to set your teeth on edge", but the appearance of Season Of Glass, *the album which followed Lennon's death, provoked an entirely different type of criticism. The LP sleeve showed John Lennon's blood smeared glasses as they were left shattered after he was attacked, while the opening track begins with gunshots, followed by Yoko screaming with terror (before she begins screaming in her attempt at singing). Another track on the record features the Lennons' son, Sean, who was five years old at the time his father was killed, reminiscing about walks he had taken with his father in New York's Central Park, and asking why anyone should want to do this to his father. It seems rather unfortunate that the boy should have been subjected to such a performance so soon (a matter of months) after the tragedy. It is difficult to reconcile this visual and aural exploitation with the image of stoic sincerity for which Yoko will be remembered from those bitter days of December 1980.*

THE CLASH ARE ONE OF THE

few British punk bands originating in the 'golden era' of punk rock to have made any inroads into stardom in the United States. Lead singer Joe Strummer (real name John Mellor) had previously been a member of a London pub rock band known as the 101'ers before joining the Clash, and one of his colleagues in the 101'ers was a native Chilean who had relocated in London with the name of Alvaro (to which he appended the interesting description 'The Chilean with the Singing Nose'). After leaving the 101'ers, Alvaro dropped from view for some time, to re-emerge in 1978 with a solo album on his own Squeaky Shoes label, whose title was Drinking My Own Sperm. We can only hope that it will eventually fertilize something. . .

Mama Cass of the Mamas and Papas
(c. Assoc Newspapers)

various audiences. No music, no singing lasting longer than a few seconds — just Elvis being sometimes patronising and often most unfunny. 'Having Fun'? In truth, the record's only redeeming feature is the fact that the sleeve proclaims with reasonable prominence 'A Talking Album Only'. All but the most ultra-masochistic Presley completists are urged to avoid this LP at all costs. . .

Then there's the rather tragic case of another rock 'n' roll casualty, Mama Cass Elliott, the well-built lady member of the Mamas and Papas, who died in London during the summer of 1974. Cass was, by all accounts, a very pleasant lady who wasn't afraid to joke about her bulk: and in fact once posed naked for the centerfold of an American magazine), but perhaps someone somewhere exceeded the bounds of propriety when a 'Best Of' collection of her work was given the title *Mama's Big Ones*. Regrettably, the kitsch elements of the unfortunate lady's life and times continued after death — a film about her life was scheduled, and the role of Mama Cass herself was offered to another quite large lady named Leah Kunkel, the wife of noted session musician Russ Kunkel. While this may seem quite reasonable, a small but vital piece of information is missing from the above. Leah Kunkel, you see, was actually Cass Elliott's sister, thus rendering the posthumous offer in extraordinarily bad taste.

Another less than sylph-like figure, ace guitarist Leslie West, who made his name as the focal point of the American hard rock group, Mountain, released a couple of solo albums during the 1970s, on one of which no less a person than Mick Jagger appeared, although as a guitarist, oddly enough. Nothing especially wrong with that, and musically the album contains nothing of which Leslie should be ashamed. The only jarring feature is the title of the record, although a tongue can be detected firmly poking through a cheek as it is decided that the album will be called *The Great Fatsby*. . .

Finally, a record which seems, in England at least, to be somewhat obscure. Whether the reader knows it or not, he or she is undoubtedly familiar with the golden-fingered hit making team of Holland, Dozier and Holland, if for no other reason than that they were responsible for helping The Supremes (later Diana Ross and the Supremes) to phenomenal record sales as songwriters and producers. Eventually the trio went their separate ways, still producing (and making hits) for a variety of artists. During the 1970s, however, one of the three, Lamont Dozier, embarked on a career as a recording artist in his own right, with moderately successful results. His inclusion here is due to the title of one of those records, which bears the exceptionally modest epithet, *Black Bach* (which, you can be sure, has nothing whatsoever to do with Wales).

There are probably innumerable LP titles

which seem to have been chosen by someone in possession of rather less sensitivity than a breeze block, but for the purposes of here and now, your attention is drawn to but four titles chosen for albums featuring far from obscure artists who were presumably aware of the travesties being perpetrated in their names.

It must be said, however, that perhaps the first and most celebrated name of this quartet may not have been aware that one of his albums boasted a title which to most people's ears seems inaccurate in the extreme. Elvis Presley's record company, even after his 1977 demise, have ensured that their main asset has a stream of new records on the market, something which has been achieved for much of the last ten years by judicious and mostly sensible and tasteful repackaging of previously issued material with a small but quite significant leavening of slightly more obscure recordings which for various reasons have not been released before. There have inevitably been occasions when good value and good taste have, perhaps inadvertently, not been considered, but one LP in particular, apart from its almost total lack of quality of any sort, bears a title which seems to lack any element of accuracy. *Having Fun With Elvis On Stage* is what the album's called, and the sound content of the record is entirely composed of Presley talking to

Leslie West

James Marshall Hendrix

JIMI HENDRIX, ALTHOUGH AN undoubtedly unique guitarist, lived briefly in the spotlight which focussed on him due to his talents. During 1981, two events have occurred which even Hendrix himself might consider excessive – the first was the release of an album featuring Jimi jamming with various other musicians, whose title was Woke Up This Morning, Found Myself Dead. A tongue may be faintly discernible in a cheek there, but the official foundation of a Jimi Hendrix Electric Church in California as a tax-exempt religious institution 'dedicated to holding jam sessions in honour of the guitarist' is enough to make Hendrix, should he somehow be aware of it, glad that he has passed on. . .

One of the most bizarre recordings

in which John Cale was involved during his time with The Velvet Underground (the group's name, by the way, came from the title of a book seen by one of the original members on a stall in Times Square subway station. The name had little significance other than that the group liked it, and no connection with the *Peyton Place* type subject matter of the novel) appeared on the group's second LP, and was titled *The Gift*. More recently, Cale described the song as "an exercise in stereo more than anything else", and there is some truth in such a description, as if the stereo balance is adjusted normally, so that both left and right sides of the recording are equally balanced, Cale's voice can be dimly heard reciting a story while engulfed by the screaming feedback noises of the rest of the group. However, if the balance control is adjusted to pick up only the side on which Cale's soft Welsh recitation is recorded, a story appears, that of Waldo Jeffers, a college student from Locust, Pennsylvania, who is not enjoying his college vacation because he has been parted from his girlfriend, Marsha Bronson, who lives in Wisconsin. Although Marsha has sworn to be faithful to Waldo, he has had bad dreams of Marsha, overcome by alcohol, submitting to the sexual embraces of "a neanderthal". Eventually, Waldo can stand this no longer, and is inspired by receiving a leaflet which has come from New York to the decision to post himself to Marsha in a large cardboard box, which he duly organizes.

Marsha, meanwhile, has indeed submitted to the desires of someone named Bill, who, far from being a neanderthal, she describes as an octopus "with arms all over the place". "However," she reports to her best friend, Sheila Klein, "he was nice about it and said he would still respect me afterwards, even though he wasn't in love with me." Eventually, after a lengthy journey in his cardboard container, Waldo is delivered to Marsha's house, where she and Sheila attempt to open it after discovering that it has been sent by Waldo, "that schmuck", as Marsha describes the unfortunate lovesick boy. The two girls are unable to lift the cardboard flap which is stapled firmly down, and after searching unsuccessfully for a pair of scissors, Marsha remembers that her father keeps several tools in a workshop in the basement, and fetches a large sheet metal cutter, with which she tries unsuccessfully, to make a slit in the cardboard. By this time, Marsha is out of breath, so Sheila has the idea of a different form of entry for the cutter. She gets on her knees, takes the tool in both hands, and plunges it into the box, through sticky tape, staples, cardboard and interior packing, and unfortunately also through Waldo's head, which we are told "split slightly". A charming record. . .

It is a reasonable and normal assumption

that any person who makes a record initially intends it to become widely heard and popular — how else, after all, can the not inconsiderable cost of recording, mastering, pressing, sleeving and all the rest be recouped other than by the record selling? However, there are a handful of artists, it would appear, who can neither understand this simple economic equation nor even know of its existence — although an alternative method of selling records (albeit not often successful, if ever) is to achieve such notoriety that a record sells via word of mouth recommendation.

One method which becomes popular from time to time is to make a record which is utterly unlikely to ever be heard in the normal course of events. One example surfaced (as in scum rising to the surface of the water) in 1978 in New York. The LP in question, which rejoiced (if that could possibly be the word) in the title *Ratfucker*, was the work of a demented songwriter/vocalist named Armand Schaubroeck, whose favourite word can be ascertained without too much trouble, as he uses it on average at least twenty times on each of the album's seven tracks. Curiously enough, much of the music (as opposed to the lyrics) on the album seems quite listenable — it's the lyrical monotony that makes it so objectionable. Presumably, Armand had convinced some other people of his genius — how else would he convince a quartet of backing singers to chant a chorus of 'I'm Fuckin' Around' on one of the less inspired tracks, *I Love Me More Than You?* He obviously also had an idea that mass acceptance would be about as simple to achieve with this record as winning the Nobel Peace Prize, as a note appears on the rear of the sleeve which reads 'I doubt if you'll ever hear this record on the radio'. Quite so . . . The album's longest track, which is quite an epic in impossibly bad taste, is *The Queen Hitter*, and appears to be about a hired killer who specializes in peforming 'contracts' on ladies whose husbands have grown tired of them.

This story does not end as simply as mercifully it might. The slightly demented record collector, who owns what must be one of the very few copies of this LP in Britain, was so fascinated by *Ratfucker* that he decided to write to its perpetrator. A few days later, the following letter was received in reply: "Thanks for writing and asking about any magazine articles about me which might exist. Peter Laughner interviewed me for *Creem* magazine — then we both decided to record the song *Queen Hitter* together. Peter's ex-wife was to play the part of the wife in *Queen Hitter*, but he went to rock 'n' roll Heaven on me". In fact, Peter Laughner, at one time member of a group from Cleveland, Ohio, who called themselves Pere Ubu, died of a drug overdose in June 1977 — this may have been the first drug-connected death of a rock critic (as opposed to musician). Armand's letter ends "If you find the time, kill me". His records are released by what must be a small label, Mirror Records of Irondequoit, New York, who also sell T shirts with the legend 'Kill Me' printed on them — one can only hope . . . that somehow he reverts to some less anti-social frame of mind.

A more recent — and European-example of this kind of thing came to light with a punkette from Germany named Nina Hagen. Not from West Germany, mind you, but originally from East Germany, whose authorities found Ms. Hagen such a disturbing presence in their 'democratic' country that they were only too happy to accede to her request to move to the capitalist world to become a rock star. First time round, Nina was a pleasant curiosity — as her lyrics

TORTURE AT 33¹⁄₃

Nina Hagen

were in German, few people in Britain had any idea of what she was singing about, and taken on a purely instrumental level, her first LP registered as a primal punk artefact, with plenty of energy and rather less expertise. It was her second LP which turned rather more stomachs, and only then because someone had decided that the lyrics to the new collection of Hagen songs, although they were still sung in German, should be printed in three languages including English on an insert to be included with the record.

It should be explained at this point that Nina had become engaged to be married around this period, her intended being pretty much a horror story on his own account. The man in question, Herman Brood, was in fact a bonafide rock superstar in his native Holland, although this status appears to have been at least partially the result of the fact that Herman was a convicted criminal and a self-confessed heroin addict. He and Nina made a lovely couple . . . but not for long, for some reason, possibly because the whole scam was only undertaken for publicity reasons (and if so, they were not too successful). Nina's second LP *Unbehagen*, contains a track whose English title is *Herman Was His Name*. Fair enough — except that the song seems to be mostly about Brood taking drugs, described in some detail:

Herman shoots up
He says to himself
That's what gets the little brainy tripping
he feels he's wise and inspired
When he gently wets his tongue
With speed.

A subsequent passage reads:
He needs the needles and the pills
To fill his veins with vital thrills
Herman's balls turn blue
He says to himself
Shit, that's all I needed, ow, owww.

Very tasteful . . . Another song on the record masquerades under the innocent title of 'Bow-Wow', while its lyrics contain the following passages:

I'm your doggie
Bit cha in the leg
And in the balls
Bite like a bastard
Chop-chop
Zap-zap
Piss all over ya
Shit on ya too
Piss a load
Wherever I can
Crap in your bed
And lick you off.

As one reviewer noted, Nina seems to have a fixation about balls, of which this is a load.

Pretending to be someone also appears

on the face of it, to be a totally pointless method of gaining attention as a rock star — presumably, the reasoning goes something like this: "If I sound very much like Joe Soap" (fill in appropriate name) "and if my record can be marketed as some kind of obscure, long lost recording, then when it becomes a hit, I can make an appearance at a dramatic unveiling ceremony, and become a star in my own right". To the uninitiated, this may seem a smart scheme — its only obvious drawback seems to be that it has been tried on several occasions, but has never actually worked. . .

Even fans of John Lennon would probably be forced to concede that the best known name in rock history is that of Elvis Presley. There have been some notable Presley impersonators who have never tried to conceal their true identity, perhaps the best one being Ral Donner, who achieved deserved fame on his own account in the early 1960s with three American top twenty hits, the first of which was a very accurate cover version of *Girl Of My Best Friend*, a song which had actually been recorded by Elvis, but only released as the B side of a Presley 45 in Britain, and apparently only as an album track in the United States. Donner's biggest hit was his follow up record, *You Don't Know What You've Got (Until You Lose It)*, which even close relations might have been hard put to deny could easily have been Elvis. But after this promising brush with the big time, Ral Donner went to ground.

Until 1980, when a double LP was released to coincide with the third anniversary of Presley's death. It was titled *1935 – 1977 (I've been away for awhile now)*. The sleeve of the album featured a drawing of Presley, and noted that the records featured Scotty Moore, D. J. Fontana and the Jordanaires, all of whom had been heavily involved in providing musical and vocal backing for Elvis records during his greatest period of influence. The fact that the record sounded uncommonly like Elvis speaking and singing, as if from the next world, was obviously something to which the record company wished to draw attention, although in fairness, a somewhat mawkish note signed by Ral Donner, which ends "If I had a wish, it would be to hear his voice again. This recording is a product of that fantasy" is also displayed on the sleeve, as is a footnote which reads "The singing and speaking voice on this recording is *not* that of Elvis Presley". No doubt the album was purchased by more than a few avid Presley fans, and in fact, most were probably quite happy even after finally discovering the small print. Not so those who bought *Don't Cry For Christmas*, a record released a year or two before the Ral Donner effort, whose label credited the song as being performed by someone called '?'. In order to establish some interest in the record, its publicist, a legendary figure in British rock 'n' roll circles known as

'Waxie Maxie', contrived to circulate the story that the track might conceivably be an undiscovered masterpiece by Elvis — it certainly could have been Elvis singing, although with an undistinguished backing and uninspired material, but insufficient quantities of the record were bought for it to have any impact.

Not long afterwards, the same record company (who were actually the British licensees for the Sun record label, on which Presley had made his earliest records) came up with another slightly dubious item, an album titled *Duets*, which was credited to Jerry Lee Lewis and Friends. Again, it was mentioned that the identity of some of the 'Friends' was uncertain, and on some tracks, there was the distinct possibility that Presley could be heard. After the fiasco with ?, few people were taken in this time, and not long afterwards the same company released a record by one Orion, apparently a Presley imitator of long standing. Two and two were put together and made four by interested parties, whereupon it became clear that in all probability both the ? single and the Presley-like voice on *Duets* were by Orion, although it should be noted that the said Orion, despite any doubts which might be raised due to his unlikely name, may not have been aware of the way in which his work was being peddled.

The same cannot unfortunately be true of a mid-'70s LP titled *Phantom's Divine Comedy Part 1*. Jim Morrison, lead singer with The Doors, is alleged to have died as a result of a heart attack in 1971, although the circumstances surrounding his disappearance, and notably the fact that no disinterested parties have ever come forward to confirm that they saw the body, have led to the possibility that Morrison went to ground. At the time of his 'death', he was awaiting trial on a charge of exposing himself during a concert, and conceivably felt that the only way to avoid becoming a public example (if guilty, he faced seven years in prison) was to disappear in as final manner as possible, without actually dying. This, of course, is all conjecture, but it was given greater impetus when *The Phantom* was released. The sleeve contained an amount of gobbledegook, and very few credits were listed which looked even faintly genuine. Phantom's vocal style was at times quite similar to the familiar Morrison tones, the sleeve showed a negative photograph of someone who could have been Jim Morrison (negatives being notoriously difficult from which to make an identification) and one of the tracks was titled *Stand Beside My Fire*. Doors aficionados will be well aware that the song with which Morrison and the group came to fame was titled *Light My Fire*, and the whole artefact seemed to be bursting with clues. Even so, the other members of the Doors have categorically denied that Phantom could possibly be Jim Morrison — the world will obviously have to wait for Morrison to return (or not) to learn the truth, but if Phantom wasn't Jim Morrison, he spent a good deal of time and money to no avail, as the album was a very poor seller.

Then there's the Klaatu case. Klaatu, in case you're wondering, was originally an alien character featured in the 1951 science fiction film *The Day The Earth Stood Still*, but a much more recent Klaatu was the name of a group which suddenly emerged to instant, if shortlived, stardom at the start of 1977. Why the fuss? To several American critics, the group sounded like The Beatles, and to deepen the mystery, Capitol Records, who released the album, claimed that they had been asked not to identify any of the musicians on it. Additionally, the group's manager refused to disclose anything about his charges, although it was discovered that he worked for EMI Records (who released Beatles discs in Britain) between 1965 and 1967, when the Beatles were extremely active, and of course Capitol Records was the company which had issued Beatle product in North America.

The group's manager obviously realized that he was involved in something with great commercial potential, and continued to feed the media with vague hints, admitting that the record was "Beatle inspired", stating that the record contained clues to the identity of the group and also drawing attention to what he termed a morse code message on the first track from the LP to be released as a single, *Sub-Rosa Subway*. In fact, the storm soon blew over, and almost the only remaining trace of Klaatu in 1981 is that one of the songs on their LP, *Calling Occupants Of Interplanetary Craft*, was covered by The Carpenters, and became a substantial hit for them. When the Klaatu LP was first released, it was accompanied by a postcard of the album's sleeve, on the back of which was written "Listen to KLAATU and know there is hope". Perhaps the final word was mis-spelt, and should have read 'hype'. . .

One of the best albums Lou Reed

has made is a double live epic (no other word is suitable) titled *Live-Take No Prisoner*, released in 1978. The album sleeve, pictured hereabouts, is fairly horrendous — one writer described it as: "presenting Lou as a faceless escapee from *Scorpio Rising* with a transvestite lower half, strutting his stuff on a garbage strewn sidewalk." Reed chose it himself: "I saw it in a magazine and right away, I knew it was an album cover. That's *exactly* how most people see Lou Reed."

One radio station employee requested a copy of the album from a representative of the record company which released the LP, and was told "I can't give you that — he says 'fuck' all the way through, and you'd be fired". As it happened, the record company man lost his job soon afterwards . . . What is on the record is a series of live versions of Reed classics, sometimes played fairly straight, but at other times containing monologs and diatribes of alarming rudeness. Reed begins the album with a curt "What's the matter? Did we keep you waiting or something?", to which an audience member complains he has had to wait outside in the rain. Rapier-like, Lou responds with "It's raining outside . . . what are you telling us for? We know it's raining outside". Then he quotes a line or two from W. B. Yeats before charging into *Sweet Jane*, which he interrupts with a speech: "Don't you hate the Academy Awards? Don't you hate fucking Barbra Streisand, thanking all the little people? Fuck short people and tall people, I like little people, people and Wyoming. Did you ever meet anyone from Wyoming? I never did." He continues with some stuff about a clerk — "I give good clerk", after which comes "I'll give you a tissue, and you can wipe my arse with it." Moving on there's a dig about Patti Smith, presumably — "Fuck Radio Ethiopia" (*Radio Ethiopia* being the title of a Patti Smith LP), "I'm Radio Brooklyn".

He interrupts a heckler with: "If you write as good as you talk, nobody reads you", a remark obviously aimed at his pet hate, the journalists, and he later refers to "evil motherfuckers" before the song grinds to a halt. During the next track, *I Wanna Be Black*, the lyrics at one point are altered to "I wanna be black like Malcolm X and have a big prick too." Curiously, the next three songs are relatively straight, before a strangely slow version of *I'm Waiting For The Man*, leavened with new lyrics like "Your mother, your father, your cock-sucking brother, they don't mean a shit to me, I don't give two shits about them, keep them away", while a later reference is to "a middle class fuck-up".

From this point on, numerous extra adjectives are added to lyrics, Lou's favorite word, apparently, being 'fucking'. But the tour de force comes in a version of the aforementioned *Walk On The Wild Side* — after lighting himself a cigarette ("I'd rather have cancer than be a faggot — that's not an anti-gay remark coming from me"), there's a fearsome passage where two New York journalists are verbally crucified, the prime remark about one of them being "What is he — a toe fucker?" Lou later explained to another journalist that he had received no law suits as a result of the record, noting "I was just expressing opinions. You still can't sue for being called a toe fucker". Continuing with the song, he then tells scurrilous stories about the characters in *Walk On The Wild Side*, the most lurid being about Candy, whom we have previously met, but who had apparently since died. "I miss Candy" says Lou "Candy Darling — caught leukaemia from a silicone tit. . . don't put plastic in your fucking tit!" And so on . . . Strangely, though, a near classic album, despite its more disgusting interludes.

Lou, talking about it later, had this to say: "In all modesty, I think that's one of the funniest albums made by a human. The record company were

---

Research for this tome has taken

place over three continents, and while Australia is light years ahead in terms of tastlessness, the strangest places throw up (the term is used advisedly) a nugget of kitsch. Miami, for instance, is apparently packed to the gills with senior citizens, and the likelihood of discovering a punk band's record on a local label, especially a band with the name of The Eat, and a label with the title Giggling Hitler Records, would normally be well worth betting against. The record is a five track mini-LP, revolving at 33⅓ rpm, and bears the title *God Punished The Fat*. It's not very good either, but a couple of the songtitles, like *Kneecappin'* and *Nut Cop* looked promising, not to mention an obviously over the top sleeve. The first of these songs has a lyric so bad it's worth quoting:

Kneecappin' My Baby and Me,
Marxist revolutionaries.
We Fire at what we see and
What we see is you talkin' back to me
Kneecappin' all over town,
Stand Up and we'll put you down
Kneecappin' and on the lam
Caught you steppin' out of your Trans-Am
Smile fades from your moustached face
As my baby puts you back in your natural place

Subtle stuff . . .

---

shocked by it, because there was no way to edit out the things that might allow that record to be played on the air. There were so many of those things that no-one would know where to start, which is why I did it really in private, and nobody got to hear it till the end. It just became an unfortunate accepted fact, but on the other hand, it was also impossible for anybody to listen to it and not fall over laughing. Between laughs, the record company would say to me "But Lou. . ." We were thinking of calling the album *But Lou*. But here's an example of the people I made this record for — once we were playing in this little hotel, and typically, they'd packed them in, over sold the house, throwing them in like so many sardines. We were getting ready to go onstage, and the air conditioning doesn't work — it's unimaginable. There are people literally hanging from the ceiling. And there's this guy sitting at a table in the front, and he takes his head and goes 'bam bam' on the table with it, and he yelled 'Take no prisoners, Lou', and that's why we gave the album that title".

Silence is
an interesting commodity

to find on a record (apart, of course, from the shiny bit in the middle, technically termed the run out groove, which is normally, but not always silent), but surprisingly, more than one record has been released of utter silence. If you think about it, there can only be a need for one silent record, as any more than that would be repetitious and even possibly plagiaristic. A recent example of the genre appeared at Christmas 1980 in the unlikely shape of an album titled *The Wit and Wisdom Of Ronald Reagan* on a previously unknown record label called Magic Records (slogan: "If it's a success, it must be magic") with a catalog number of ABRA 1. One side of the LP was devoted to the then President-elect's wit, the other to his wisdom, and it would hardly take an Einstein to discover at some speed that both sides were entirely silent. The album, by the way, retailed at around $5, (and in Britain for £2) and presumably copies were offered for sale and purchased, despite the fact that the notion of *buying* silence appears perverse to say the least.

Or is it? During the latter half of the 1970s, a small Californian record company known as Beserkeley (they were based in the Berkeley area and boasted the corporate slogan: 'Fun, fun, fun, till they take the keys away') released a single by an artist widely presumed to be the company, masquerading under the name Son Of Pete. The first side of the record contained a song titled *Silent Knight* — not that it made too much difference as the other side, *Disco Party Part Two*, sounded distinctly similar to the 'A' side, and both sounded distinctly silent. On this occasion, the joke was carried even further, as both sides credited and arranger, a producer and even a remix engineer, but that wasn't all — the record was supplied to juke boxes in the Berkeley area and allegedly became a very popular item in certain bars and roadhouses were juke boxes supplied an unceasing diet of rock music; the staff of these establishments willingly payed their dimes and nickels to free themselves from the pandemonium to which they were normally subjected. Incidentally, Son Of Pete is also presumed to be the same individual as that legendary band who recorded for the Organ label, the Muffdivers, whose only known release was a single, *Saga Of Yukon Pete*, which gourmets of bad taste may recognize as a sequel to the more celebrated *Eskimo Nell*. It is hardly stretching a point to describe this opus as utterly filthy, a judgment reinforced by the twelve page booklet accompanying the reord which illustrates the 'saga' in perfectly appalling graphic cartoons — this record is perhaps the ultimate trough of kitsch, and therefore, it goes without saying highly prized, a collector's item.

Reverting to the idea of silence (a topic which will seem doubly appealing should you ever be unwittingly subjected to *Yukon Pete*), no less a person than the late John Lennon was able to appreciate the virtue of this priceless commodity. On his 1973 album *Mind Games*, Lennon and his wife, Yoko, declared the birth of what they termed a 'conceptual country' which would be known as Nutopia. Among other things, the Lennons informed us that Nutopia had 'no land, no boundaries, no passports, only people' and 'no laws other than cosmic'. As a result, it was no real surprise that the final track on the first side of the album, *Nutopian International Anthem*, should consist of ten seconds of unsullied vinyl.

The question of why artists find it necessary to devote any physical part of a record to silence brings to mind another similar case, that of Woodstock heroes, Sly and the Family Stone. The group's enormously successful 1971 LP, *There's a Riot Goin' On*, enjoyed almost unanimous critical acclaim, but with one notable exception — both the album's sleeve and its label listed the title track, but no such track was present on the disc. This was presumed to be faintly amusing by the vast majority of those who purchased the record, but one person was so upset by the track's absence that she took the matter to court, and logically enough, won the case. It has been said, probably apocryphally, that this case inspired the writing of the song *Man Smart, Woman Smarter . . .*

Pure, unadulterated
crudity is a commodity

rarely found on vinyl, which in many ways is just as well, as there appears to be enough trouble in the world without the aural equivalent of live pornography, with its attendant audience of grey middle aged men who wear long raincoats and spend long hours watching elderly boilers making unpleasant spectacles of themselves in sleazy basements where even the spiders are syphilitic.

Any survey of the best of the worst in rock would be incomplete, however, without at least a brief reference to a few of these nauseous discs, starting with the most obscure of the trio which immediately come to mind, a four track record the size of a single but designed to revolve at the lower speed of an album. The group responsible for this outrage were known as The Gizmos, who recorded for a label from Bloomington, Indiana, called Gulcher Records, which was probably also the name of a local rock magazine. One of the group's members may have been Richard Meltzer, one of America's more bizarre rock writers — Meltzer published a strange book, *The Aesthetics Of Rock*, in 1970, and its more than three hundred pages have remained a total mystery to just about everyone who has ever tried to read it. As one rock historian noted: "This makes *Finnegan's Wake* seem like *Snoopy* — everyone knows most of the words, but it's the order he puts them in, and the overall context,

Sly Stone

Country Joe Macdonald

which makes the book so difficult to understand."

For the reader's edification, there follows a short passage selected at random from the volume: "But usually the Beach Boys soar to the heights of freedom through aloofness from the material basis of arrogance; 'Fun, Fun, Fun' described their freedom before, during and after the loss of possession." That, of course, says it all – but all what?

To return to the subject of The Gizmos, Meltzer wrote a sleeve note to the record in question, of which the following are some of the more illuminating excerpts: "Yeah, they're growing a new generation of he-men in Indiana these days . . . now they're producing REAL MEN who don't mind one bit if the cranny they're porking gets to come too. In fact these guys more or less *prefer* it and they ain't even askin' that the gammar gobble their prod first: 'Let her know she's your favourite gal, stick your tongue in her birth canal.'" Surprisingly enough, this is actually a reasonable relevant introduction to one of the tracks on the record, *Muff Divin' (In Wilkie South)*, which seems to be a kind of recorded cunnilingus instruction course. A brief snatch of the lyrics will probably suffice at this point – the lyrics certainly don't get any better than this, that's for sure . . .

'Muff Divin' in the Willkie South,
Spread her legs and open your mouth.
Puff your lips and make a ridge.
Get some ketchup from the fridge.
Try to go and seek her out,
Make sure you take your dentures out.
Don't kiss your babe,
Don't touch her tits,
Just get right down and lick her . . .

By now even the least imaginative person has probably got the picture . . .

'Country' Joe McDonald was the leader of an excellent psychedelic band from San Francisco, Country Joe and The Fish, a group which made what is unarguably one of the finest albums of the late 1960s, or of any other period you care to mention. It is the opinion of most rock fans that this LP, *Electric Music For The Mind and Body* achieved a standard of brilliance which Joe has never been able to regain, either with The Fish or as a solo recording artist. Perhaps, however, the nadir of his career came in

1971, when Joe was invited to produce some original songs for the soundtrack of a particularly explicit movie, *Quiet Days in Clichy*, Henry Miller's story of two students in Paris shortly before the outbreak of the Second World War. It is supposedly autobiographical, which would appear to mean that Henry quite enjoyed himself as an American in Paris. Joe McDonald wrote a title song for the film (which, not at all incidentally, was directed by Jens Jorgen Thorsen, who much more recently created a completely understandable furore when he announced his intention of making a film in England about Christ, in which Jesus was portrayed as a homosexual). Obviously, *Clichy* was just a test run at that rate, although Joe's lyrics pulled no punches at all, as will become rapidly clear.

> Come on people and listen to me,
> I'll tell you the story of Carl and Joey,
> The girls they fucked and the women they laid,
> This is the story of the love they made.
> Now don't get excited, be patient, please,
> Just put your hand on your lover's knee,
> And during the movie, if you get the chance,
> Put your hand inside her pants.

Some might consider this advice eminently reasonable, but it certainly didn't help the movie gain a wide release. The song is repeated during the film, this time with even more explicit lyrics — 'We took both of them to our flat, and the red-haired one gave Carl the clap. He tried everything, but just his luck, The one from Jamaica just wouldn't fuck' . . . and it gets worse.

It has to be said that both The Gizmos and Country Joe made records which were nothing short of grossly offensive — there is little or no art in lyrics as explicit as these, by the same token which makes a partially clothed body so much more exciting than a totally naked one. The virtue of subtlety is one that has obviously eluded both singer and group, and they would seem to deserve our sympathy at least as much as our contempt.

It doesn't take much research to

realize that group names, as discussed elsewhere, are as often chosen for their ability to outrage as for any socially redeeming qualities; a typically boorish example is that of The Incredible Simon Stokes and the Black Whip Thrill Band, whose one and only LP under this handle was released in 1973. In fact, the band who released an album for a record company, whose management (old stiffs that they were) refused to allow Simon Stokes to call his cohorts the Black Whip Thrill Band, as a result of which the LP was released under the positively tedious name of Simon Stokes and the Nighthawks. Stokes once explained that he thought that the Black Whip Thrill Band "was what rock 'n' roll is all about. It has that element of . . . you know, I think you're dead the minute a kid's mother says O.K., you can watch this group. I think that's your first downfall. Secondly, they say 'Can you hear this record, Mr Stokes?' Start calling you Mister, and you're in trouble".

Prior to this album, Stokes had been part of a group with the equally unlikely name of Rock Bottom and the Candy Kisses, who scored a minor hit with a song titled *Candy Is Dandy But Love Don't Rot Your Teeth*, among other less notable aggregations, but his the Black Whip Thrill Band was the album which he felt would really make him a star (well, Simon, *this* is your life!). "The idea came from an old magazine, which Sears wouldn't carry — stores wouldn't put it in their racks. I think it's quite humorous, and it was meant to be humorous, but nobody saw the humor but me. I always think of these people that see it, go home and play it, and beat up the whole household and stuff, but it really wasn't meant for that. I really like the monks — there's nothing more fiendish than a fiendish monk!"

Whatever else he may have done, Simon Stokes did not deserve these words from a churlish reviewer of one of his gigs: "'looking terribly similar to Charles Manson, Simon Stokes and the Nighthawks. . ." As Stokes himself remarked: "Once a review starts like that, nobody's going to like you. It's like saying 'If Jack the Ripper were reincarnated, you are him'." It might be true, but does it give a guy a sporting chance? The Nighthawks, aka The Black Whip Thrill Band themselves were apparently hardly the types you'd meet at vicarage tea parties — "They were just fucking awful. We fought among ourselves, because it was a violent group anyway. I'm probably the least violent in the group, but the whole group tended towards violence, and I never knew when there'd be fist fights just before going on stage. And the bass player was prone to walking off stage and saying 'Fuck you' to the crowd, which would get us in trouble all the time." Simon also remembers an occasion which seems worth documenting, although it would no doubt be improved by some visual accompaniment, which unfortunately doesn't exist.

Nowadays, I've lost a lot of weight, but when we played at the Whiskey A Go Go in Los Angeles, reviews were calling me obese and I sort of felt like I had Mick Jagger's mind in Orson Welles' body. And one time when I was really heavy, the Nighthawks played at this afternoon festival, and it was the height of peace and love, and everybody was doing peace signs. Everybody hated each other, but they were saying 'I love you', and all the hostilities were held back. I had never been there before, and for some reason I has the idea that it was going to be really classy. So I bought this suit, tailored sort of Tom Jones type suit with red, white and blue stripes, with a waistcoat that tied at the front. I had really gotten heavy since I bought the suit, due to the frustations

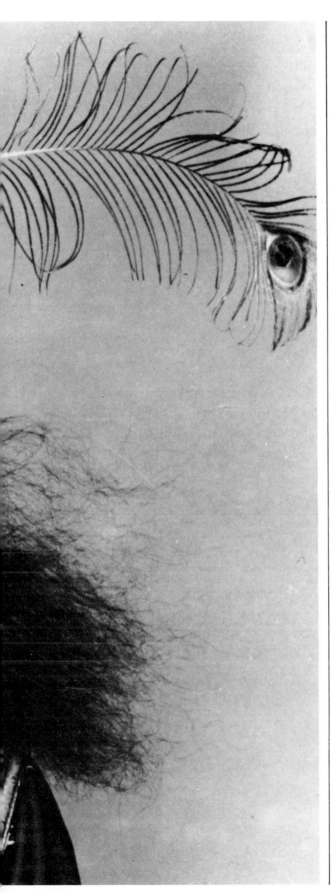

Simon Stokes

which led me to drinking all day and not caring about anything … But I said to myself, 'I'm going to knock this audience dead', and I put on the suit and the pants — and when you're really heavy, you can hardly get into your clothes, and I'm hanging out of the side. I've got this fancy thing on, and I'm trying not to move, because if I do, I'll split it! And I'd been drinking anyway and I didn't know where half the band was, they'd disappeared. When I got on stage, everybody else was in T shirts, the audience and the rest of the group, and I come out looking like a really overweight Tom Jones. It was really the worst time — and to top it all off, everybody was into peace and love, and we were singing motorcycle songs. The audience just hated me! They're booing us, and we're stomping around, some guy got on stage and was going to hit one of the members of the band — it was just awful. And I was getting scared of being lynched, because there was no way out — our track was there, but I couldn't get away because it was an oval field and the audience was blocking the exists. When we got offstage finally, there was this midget with a hunched back and a cape waiting for me, with a whole bunch of bikers behind him, and I thought 'Oh no! What now?' But the midget comes up to me and says 'Man, that was the best act we've seen since Alice Cooper,' and I breathed again. But I was very worried there for a while.

There is a curious coda to this story, which concerns the music on the Black Whip Thrill Band record. Despite the monks operating the rack and torturing the nubiles, in musical terms, the album is little short of excellent. While songs like *Ride On Angel*, which deals with a murder in a bar committed by Hell's Angels, seem on the face of it to be gratuitously praising violence, Stokes' eventual intentions were that it should be heard as a protest against the death penalty — at the time the song was recorded the death penalty in America stood in abeyance, which resulted in any prisoners waiting on Death Row being unable to discover whether they were going to be executed. Another song, *The Ballad Of Lennie and George,* is based on the story in John Steinbeck's classic novel, *Of Mice And Men*, and is actually very moving. Of course, there are the less serious songs like *The Boa Constrictor Ate My Wife Last Night* and another tongue in cheek epic *I Fell For Her, She Fell For Him, He Fell For Me,* the ramifications of which are certainly quite confusing. If Simon is still around, he would appear to be perfectly in tune with a good deal of the music being made in the 1980s, and many worse things could happen than another Stokes record being released. Stokes may well feel justified in believing that he was just ahead of his time — isn't that always the way?

MEET THE PUBLIC – on tour and in performance

Without much doubt, one of the more colorful figures in the history of rock music is Iggy Pop, who has been creating various kinds of interesting havoc ever since the first time he and his first and most famous group, the Stooges, began their performing career in Detroit during 1968. Iggy, whose parents called him James Osterberg, was brought up in a caravan park, and played drums with a school band called the Iguanas (from which, of course, came his nickname). After adolescent dalliances with careers as a golf professional and/or life saver, Iggy discovered his true vocation as a singer shortly before his twenty first birthday, and the initial Stooges gig featured Iggy playing both Hawaiian guitar and vacuum cleaner. Iggy himself recalled how this led to his being offered his first recording contract: "I had a maternity dress on and a white face, and I was doing unattractive things like spitting on people. Then, just like in the movies, this guy came up to me and said 'You're a star'".

While the Stooges were very inspirational musically (or, as some critics have intimated, so loud that there was no future in failing to enjoy them – if you're about to have your eardrums perforated, you might as well have a smile on your face), much of their appeal was in Iggy's uninhibited stage presence, which tended either to inflame or totally alienate his audiences. A particular speciality of those heady days was when Iggy would allow hot candle wax to run over his usually bare chested body, or smash himself in the mouth with his microphone, incurring the kind of damage which must have kept his dentist in lox for life.

Another favorite Iggy trick was to approach an unsuspecting couple in the audience and scream maniacally into their faces before smashing the microphone against his own lip to draw blood and ending with an angelic smile, the prelude to pushing the mike down the front of his trousers and then pushing it inches away from the face of his victims.

Quite a charmer, our Iggy, he was the only pre-punk who picked his nose on stage and removed imaginary hairs from his backside, presenting them to the favored front row of the audience. One of his more memorable exploits concerned a reviewer from Billboard – during the course of his performance, Iggy sat on the reviewer's lap, put his arms around the unfortunate scribe, and pretended to go to sleep with his head on Mr Billboard's shoulder. A review in Cashbox magazine in 1970 indicates that this kind of behavior was all in a day's work for Mr Pop: "Audience reaction ranged from vague amusement to sheer terror. Iggy writhed on the floor, tore at his bare chest with his long fingernails and danced on the tables, kicking drinks, ashtrays and other paraphernalia into people's laps."

All this suffering for the sake of art couldn't go on indefinitely – apart from the physical torture through which Iggy put himself every night, the mental strain on members of his band was too much to take. Iggy himself spent some time in mental institutions, while various other Stooges were less fortunate. Bass player Dave Alexander contracted an infected pancreas, caught pneumonia and died, while his successor,

Zeke Zettner, overdosed on heroin, and almost every other Stooge has at one time or another come close to death as a result of severe drug addiction. Almost the only Stooge to survive apparently none the worse for wear has been Iggy himself, who continues to make exceptionally good records from time to time, although nowadays without the other Stooges.

The recorded legacy of The Stooges is in general highly listenable, although what might have passed for a good standard was kicked in the teeth by the release of a recording of the group's final concert. Apart from low fidelity in musical terms, Iggy is less than subtle in his vocal performance, introducing among other gems a song "which was co-written by my mother" entitled *I've Got My Cock In My Pocket*. With a scream of "One, two, fuck you pricks!", Iggy launches into a song whose most imaginative line appears to be "I just want to fuck". Several tracks are equally subtle, and at one point, Iggy asks the audience whether they have anything *else* left to throw at him, even encouraging a particular member of the crowd to throw another egg, because he missed with the first one. It is pleasing to be able to report that five years later, Iggy was able to boast: "I was rich in the good name I'd built up for myself by fulfilling my obligations, which is something I heartily advise any young musician or singer to do." And this is the same person, who at the end of that final Stooges fiasco, addressed a member of his audience thusly: "Thank you very much to the person who threw this glass bottle at my head. It nearly killed me, but you missed again. Come back and try again next week." Although Iggy didn't know it at the time, there wouldn't be a next week. And one disappointed fan still roams the streets, with a bottle.

Iggy Pop

A RECORD PRODUCER TELLS THE STORY

of why Ry Cooder, now a world famous guitar player, but some years ago a member of the Magic Band, as Beefheart referred to his backing group, finally left the Captain's employ: "The band did a gig in San Francisco outdoors during the Haight Ashbury days, and Ry went into the desert, where Beefheart lives, to collect him. The story Ry tells is that when he arrived at the house, Captain Beefheart was still in bed, so Ry said: "Come on Don, it's time for us to go". Beefheart replied: "But first I must take a shower", which he did, but then he put his clothes straight on without drying himself. Then he got in the car and said: "We can't go – I feel clammy all over', and Ry reminded him that he hadn't dried off, so he dried himself and felt better, more relaxed. By this time, Ry was getting really uptight, and he said that they got on the stage with all the hippies in the audience with their incense, having fun. Beefheart came on stage, and just as the band was announced, he turned around to look at Ry, put his hand over his heart and said: "My heart! My heart!", and walked off the stage, leaving them all standing there. Ry never saw him again".

Ry Cooder

Cale

During 1977, while playing a concert

in London, John Cale achieved real notoriety when he sliced the head off a live chicken on stage, an act which was met by almost equal portions of horror and ecstasy by his audience.

Cale, formerly of The Velvet Underground, recently denied that one concert he staged included an item where a grand piano was smashed to pieces on stage (in the name of art!) but confirmed that on another occasion, during an avant garde music festival he helped to organize at Goldsmith's College in London (which he was due to leave on the following day), he staged a piece where a potted plant was put on stage, and a performer was supposed to scream at it until it died: "That was my parting gesture to Goldsmith's, and the festival contained several Dada pieces. The plant didn't die — it would have taken a long time — but it was a resounding performance. Robin Page, the performer, started screaming up in the corridors around the great hall — you could hear this screaming from somewhere else in the building getting nearer and nearer, but the mistake he made was to enter the hall itself. As long as he stayed out there, he didn't know what was going on, so he walked in to the hall, through the swing doors, just like a sheriff walking into a saloon and he blew it".

Cale once defined his avant garde performances as "fun with money", and if reports are correct, this was never more true than when one of his later collaborators, another avant garde musician named LaMonte Young, recorded an album of which one hundred copies were pressed which were to be sold at a price of two thousand dollars each. Cale commented: "He didn't tell me he was charging two thousand dollars per album, he said it was something like three hundred". Young also at one time distributed one of his LPs solely through art galleries . . .

Asked on one occasion what was the attraction of the avant garde, Cale replied: "There seemed to be a lot of energy — these Koreans and Japanese, and it was a pretty violent form of political mindset that was going on there. There was a Lithuanian with no passport, a Korean who was writing pieces that gave instructions like "Climb into the vagina of a live female whale" and Yoko Ono. I would imagine that the State Department was less than amused by these characters crawling around . . . Then I was in a group called the Dream Syndicate, which consisted of LaMonte Young, his wife, a violin player named Tony, and myself. Tony and I played amplified stringed instruments, a violin and a viola, and LaMonte started off with a saxophone initially, but because the music itself was just intonation, he was forced away from the saxophone, because that system was out of tune. So he and his wife began singing, and the concerts we gave consisted of holding one chord for forty five minutes — it was a form of sensory deprivation for all concerned".

The Stranglers (previously known as

the Guildford Stranglers, as that was the city in which the band first came together) have had a checkered career, to say the least, peppered with legal souffles which many observers consider were, at least part of the time, pre-meditated and successful attempts to attract the attention of the national, as opposed to purely musical, media. Being banned by the Greater London Council for wearing T shirts with slogans of a supposedly risqué and possibly obscene nature was just one occasion among many brushes with the law over the years, while three of the four group members faced prison sentences in Europe for allegedly inciting a riot at one point. One of the band's least meaningful outbursts came when they were booked to appear on a television program, *Rock Goes To College*, which on this particular occasion was to be filmed at the University of Surrey, coincidentally sited in Guildford. Eye witnesses confirm that the group behaved normally until the cameras began to capture the event, whereupon the Stranglers began to destroy their equipment, in protest, they later said, at the fact that their audience was composed for the most part of students, the general public being barred from the performance. It seems unlikely that the Stranglers will be seen on television, or at least on BBC television, for some considerable time, if they are ever allowed on the small screen again.

During 1980, lead singer Hugh Cornwell (or 'old chicken legs', as early fans of the band called him), was arrested with a concert promoter after a search for possession of various drugs about his person, and Cornwell served a three month prison sentence, since which time the group have confined themselves to less high profile mayhem. During 1981, for instance, they were rarely seen in Britain, and were apparently concentrating on making along overdue impact in the United States. . . The particular episode which seems to deserve inclusion in this volume occurred in 1978, on the occasion of the release of the band's third LP, which was titled *Black and White*. Attempts were made to press the record in black and white vinyl to produce an effect of a series of concentric and contrasting circles as the disc revolved, but at the time of release, this proved technologically impossible. However, the album was supposed to represent extreme contrasts (hence the title), and in order to effectively launch it, United Artists, who were releasing the record, organized a plane lift of around forty media and record company personnel to Iceland, conveniently an island which was fairly accessible, and one which was also eager to enhance its tourist trade, and would grant financial concessions relating to both travel and accommodation in the hope that a corps of journalists from other countries would write in attractive terms about their volcanic – well, paradise was the word they were hoping would be used,

The Stranglers

although in the event, the extraordinary bleakness of the place, and the highly disorienting twenty one hours per day of daylight at the time of the visit, seemed to suggest very different concepts to the writers who made the trip.

The individual who became the star of this expedition was not one of the Stranglers, but in fact, one of the journalists who made the trip. Not normally accustomed to reporting events with a musical bias, he was employed in a freelance capacity by one of the then pair of London evening newspapers, and was invited to become a member of the party when the paper's habitual music writer found himself over-committed. Seemingly, no-one else on the Icelandair plane to Keflavik had previously met this celebrity (as he became), although Nigel, as we shall call him, made an instant impression when he arrived at Heathrow sporting a silver topped cane and a limp, the latter, he claimed, acquired in an accident with a skateboard (these dangerous appliances were at the time enjoying their brief vogue in Britain). The outward flight was free of any untoward incident, while the tedious coach trip through the bleak larva strewn Icelandic 'countryside' was equally of little note. The party then installed themselves in what was described as the finest hotel in Reykjavik, the largest conurbation and captial city of Iceland. The Hotel Loftleider was seemingly unexceptional – quite extensive, of course, and not dissimilar from the more familiar concept of a Holiday Inn, and with the added cachet of having been the venue for the remarkable World Chess Championship Final between Bobby Fischer and Boris Spassky of Russia a few years previously. After settling in to their rooms, the Stranglers party were appraised of the excitements which awaited them – a visit to the one and only recording studio in Iceland, where a press conference would take place, was the first of these. Reportedly, the Stranglers were not exceptionally communicative to the Icelandic Press, and the visit became considerably enlivened with the introduction of lethal cocktails specially prepared for this momentous occasion. It became clear that while the incidence of even the smallest quantity of marijuana and/or cocaine in Iceland was akin to discovering oil in one's back garden (this fact being explained by the country's geographic location – totally surrounded by water, and with little communication with territories where drugs are easily obtainable), the average Icelander's ingenuity at producing mind- and body-curdling alcoholic concoctions needs to be sampled to be believed.

The still broad daylight of what was normally considered the evening, therefore, passed in quiet contemplation and the consumption of still more alcohol – the record company had been alerted in advance that the price of alcoholic beverages from the hotel or any other licensed premise would be alarming, an example being that a single gin and tonic would cost approximately $10, or that sum's equivalent in kroner, the local currency, and as a result, had given some members of the party a not insubstantial sum which they were to spend on liquor at the Keflavik duty free shop. It later transpired that over 70% of the population of Iceland left the country at least once a year, not, it was said, because they particularly wished to go anywhere, but rather in order that they should be able to replenish their personal wine cellars at reasonable prices.

Then came the day of the concert which the Stranglers were giving at a hall with a capacity of approximately five thousand people. There was great excitement among the rock afficionados of Iceland, as the Stranglers were apparently only the third British group to appear in the country during the 1970s, previous visits having been made several years before by Slade and, curiously, Led Zeppelin. That the

THE ULTIMATELY DISTURBING ASPECTS *of heavy metal bands dabbling in black magic were graphically demonstrated by an (at the time) up and coming group of headbangers with the ill-chosen name of Witchfynde. One Friday the 13th (it says here), the group discovered that they were indebted to their record company to the tune of £25,000 (although there have been no explanations as to how this large sum was amassed). They were also finding problems with their amplification system, necessitating lengthy gaps between their gigs being organized, and on the said Friday, the band had thought that they might be making a significant step forward with the broadcasting of a live session on BBC Radio One. This eventually occurred, although not without their tape failing to play three times. On the same night, the band were playing a gig, and their manager found them huddled around a table in a darkened room lit by a single candle, although no explanation was offered for this behavior. When the band eventually took the stage, every piece of amplification equipment the band possessed broke down simultaneously.*

Next day, the band's manager received a call from the guitarist's mother, who had found her son shaking in bed, while the wife of the singer also called to report that her husband, along with the band's drummer, had disappeared. The manager propounded the theory that the missing duo had contacted the coven of which they were both members, and various pleas for the missing pair to reveal their whereabouts were broadcast.

A few days later, the manager's suspicions were confirmed, when the singer and drummer contacted their manager, explaining that they had been involved in magic rites from which they could not be disturbed. They also (and this is exceedingly upsetting) suggested that the illness of their guitarist was probably the result of their actions. Oh, the trials and tribulations of the music business.

hall was completely sold out in advance of the performance became doubly impressive when it was learnt that the population of Reykjavik was a little over eighty thousand people — five thousand of them attending a Stranglers concert amounted to between six and seven per cent of the city's entire population, a remarkable statistic in any terms.

The concert was apparently relatively straightforward, and presumably regarded as quite successful, after which the visiting party adjourned to a local night club/discotheque, which, it was stated, would be emptied of its normal clientele before the party arrived. However, this did not seem to be the case — a milling throng clustered around the club's entrance, refusing all polite entreaties to go home, after which a terrifying and bloody riot broke out, watched from a distance by the less than intrepid journalists. After

Teddy Pendergrass

standing around outside in the still bright light of midnight (a local inhabitant was asked what happened in Iceland during the half of the year when darkness engulfed the country for nine tenths of each day, replied "It's very simple. In the summer, like now, we fish and we fuck. In the winter, it's too dark to fish"), the party cautiously moved into the night club, witnessing a few more brutal encounters between ordinary customers and bouncers, and proceeded to drink themselves into a state close to oblivion courtesy of various journalistic tricks learned during years of freeloading.

But we must return to the subject of this essay, Nigel. Having consumed enough alcohol of various types to inebriate a medium sized elephant, he began to 'score', as he termed it. Another alarming statistic coming to light around this time was that the population of Iceland was not split equally to produce 50% men and 50% women, but that there were rather more females than males in general circulation. This in itself sounded like good news to Nigel and one or two others in the party, particularly when a rider to this information also became known — that a somewhat high percentage of Icelandic males were actually homosexuals! Wasting no time, Nigel made himself known to an Icelandic lady, and within minutes, the two had disappeared.

About one hour later, Nigel reappeared, alone, and proceeded to engage another unfortunate native lady in conversation. Within a few minutes, he again disappeared. Nigel wasn't seen again until the next morning, although the writer who was unlucky enough to be quartered in the room next door to Nigel's was alarmed to be awoken from his drunken stupor only, it seemed, five minutes after he had found his way back to the Loftleidir and pulled the blankets over his head to extinguish the ever bright daylight. Discovering his telephone with some difficulty, the writer dialled the number of the room next door, and in some alarm, inquired whether Nigel was 'all right'. "Perfectly, old boy", boomed the Wodehousian tones at the other end of the phone. "Sorry if I woke you, but this filly I've got here was a bit close to the wall, and while we were enjoying each other, her head was banging against this partition", which he hammered

BLACK SOUL STAR
TEDDY PRENDERGRASS

(most famous as the lead voice on several hits by Harold Melvin and the Blue Notes) was able simultaneously to enhance his appeal to one section of his audience while seriously jeopardizing his popularity with another section as a result of a particular decision, the ramifications of which were that he would play a series of concerts to which only females would be admitted.

on loudly to underline the point. "Yes", he continued, "It's been quite a tiring night, though – this is the third girl I've had in here tonight". Curiously, enough eye-witnesses had seen Nigel commuting between the hotel and the night club to support his story, and when he arrived in the hotel dining room for breakfast, a respectful hush came over the other members of the party boasting about the extent of their hangovers.

Oddly enough, worse was to follow, it is reported. Although the party was due to depart during the afternoon of the day following the concert, further entertainment had been planned: the visitors would be transported into the more rural outskirts of Reykjavik, where they would be shown around a pumping station – being a volcanic island, Iceland is fortunate to be able to heat each residence on the peninsula naturally, with the hot water from the sulphur springs which occur organically in a volcanic earth formation. While inspecting the pipe systems which warmed a large part of the island, the party would also be introduced to the Mayor of Reykjavik, who would serve whisky laced with natural spring water. Nigel was near the front of the line for the whisky, returning several times to reportedly insure that the proportion of alcohol in his bloodstream was topped up, after which a final 'treat' took place for the visitors – they were given the chance to ride small and apparently innocuous looking Icelandic ponies. It became quickly clear that no-one had explained to the beasts that the passengers they were about to carry were regarded as important by the Iceland Bureau of Tourism, and within seconds, half a dozen confused writers were wondering why they had been deposited unceremoniously on the ground seconds after mounting their Thelwellesque steeds. Two other journalists were, if anything, less fortunate – the correspondent from one British muisc paper was on a pony which apparently wished to return to the mountains from which it had originally been removed, and headed for them at a gallop, being lost to view in a matter of seconds. Fortunately, a search party recovered horse and rider an hour later. The other part time equestrian was less fortunate – after a comparatively sedate, if bumpy ride. The pony suddenly seemed to decide that it no longer enjoyed bearing a passenger, and deposited him, after a hair-raising sprint followed by an astonishingly abrupt stop, into a pile of gravel, many fragments of which had to be removed from the writer's cranium over the following days. For his part, Nigel enjoyed a trouble free ride, although it was later rumored that he had become friendly with the coach driver, and had persuaded that worthy to allow him to sample some of the almost pure alcohol which the driver mixed with grapefruit juice to concoct a kamikaze cocktail, on which Nigel later blamed his subsequent misfortunes. . .

Boarding the coach for the journey back to Keflavik airport, Nigel, suddenly mindful of the fact that he had put his thirst and carnal desires higher on his scale of preferences than actually acquiring enough informa-

tion to write a story in his paper, began an animated conversation with Stranglers bass player/vocalist Jean-Jacques Burnel (John to his friends). Regrettably, Burnel was at the time consuming a bottle of some kind of alcoholic spirit, and in the interests of a good journalist/performer relationship, Nigel offered to help him finish it.

The journey on the coach was due to take about one hour, but the nursing of the mental and physical injuries which afflicted almost everyone on the trip was interrupted when Nigel suddenly lurched from his seat, seized the coach's public address system from the astonished driver, and began to propound his theories concerning the Stranglers, the music business, and just about everything else he could think of, liberally leavening his speech with language which would only very rarely be heard in polite society. After some ten minutes of Nigel's tirade, he collapsed as if poleaxed shortly before the coach pulled up alongside the airport terminal. After a vain attempt by record company personnel to convince Nigel that he must start trying to behave like a relatively normal person, it was discovered that he was completely unconscious, and a wheelchair was brought to the coach.

However primitive the population of Iceland may appear to the reader, their airline officials can detect an unconscious drunk, and Nigel was not permitted to board the aeroplane which would be transporting the by now semi-numb party back to London. The Stranglers, however, being the pleasant individuals they are, made no objection to posing around Nigel, as the latter lay slumped in his wheelchair, dead to the world, clutching an empty bottle thoughtfully placed in his hand by one of the assembled company. The writer who recounted this strange story (and who could not believe that truth is without doubt stranger than fiction?) adds that it should not be assumed by any means that all press 'junkets' to foreign countries organized by the music business will turn out to be quite as spectacularly memorable as the trip with the Stranglers to Iceland. . .

EARLY SEX PISTOLS' GIGS WERE inclined to deteriorate into a shambles, as an eye-witness of an early performance at the 100 Club Recalled: "Glen Matlock decided mid-set that he'd had enough of John's singing out of tune, and told him so in no uncertain terms. John retaliated by pulling over Paul's cymbals, so Paul rushed off and demolished the dressing room, and Steve broke all the strings on his guitar".

BETTE MIDLER, THE AMERICAN cabaret performer who starred in the notable rock film, The Rose, was not always noted for her ability as a straightforward (and not untalented) actress and singer. During a performance at the London Palladium in 1978, Bette regaled her adoring audience with some spoken material between songs which might have brought a flush to the face of a marble statue. The other protagonist in these cameos was none other than Sophie Tucker's (presumably fictitious) boyfriend Ernie: – "I was in bed the other night with Ernie, and he said 'Hey, you know you've got a tight box and no tits', and I said 'Get off my back, Ernie'." The audience were reportedly in fits . . . and then "I said to my boyfriend Ernie 'I want to kiss me where it smells'. So he drove me to Wapping". Having read these brief excerpts from Ms. Midler's repertoire, it may be difficult for the reader to take seriously any further examples of her singing, and perhaps some people may regard her in a somewhat different light – as Lou Reed might say, as a sewer guard . . .

Bette Midler

The Runaways

THE RUNAWAYS WERE AN ALL GIRL five piece band discovered and initially produced by Kim Fowley, whose flair for publicity has surely entitled him to claim to be semi-legendary. The relationship between Fowley and the group was briefly quite successful, although the five girls obviously learned a good deal from him about the value of publicity, as evidenced by these quotes: "I think about fucking a lot when I play my guitar" (by Lita Ford), and "Bass Players have a problem — everything vibrates and pretty soon you can't jump about any longer, because you desperately need to urinate" (Jackie Fox). For better or worse, the Runaways' fast growing ability to generate column inches for themselves was rarely followed by mammoth record sales, but not too long after it became obvious that the band was unlikely to happen in a big way, they fell out with Fowley, who had this to say about their lead singer: "Handling Cherie Curie's ego is like having a dog urinate in your face". Bodily functions rule, OK, but the Runaways just faded away.

The world appears to be full of erstwhile

road managers, undoubtedly in most cases at the height of their chosen profession, but who will regale anyone who cares to listen (and this is particularly true if the person listening happens to be a journalist) with imaginative thoughts concerning situations, generally of a sexual nature, in which they have found themselves. No minority group is safe from inclusion in these epics — amputees, transvestites, urolagniacs. It's like a television quiz titled 'What's Your Fetish?' most of the time when a journalist is either so inexperienced or simple minded to report these ultimately hyperbolic fantasies in print.

However, there is one tour manager who can justifiably claim to have a genuinely nasty story to tell, although to meet him, it would be quite difficult to imagine his part in the events in which he was a central figure. This gentleman's name in Phillip Clark Kautman, who, almost inevitably, is American. His early years were spent in the film industry as an extra, but this somewhat nebulous 'career' was nipped in the bud when he was sentenced to several years imprisonment as a result of his use of marijuana. This was, of course, some years ago, and it is probably accurate to suggest that the penalty for his crime, had he committed it today, would be little more than a small fine . . . However, his prison term brought Phil into contact with one Charles Manson (this was before Manson's foundation known as 'The Family', members of which, under Manson's instructions, killed Roman Polanski's wife, Sharon Tate, in horrifying circumstances). At the point when he met Kaufman, Manson was serving a brief sentence for some far lesser crime, and the two became friendly, to the point where Kaufman offered to assist Manson in the latter's attempts to become a recording artist. This help took the form of introducing Manson to a friendly manager of a recording studio, and assisting with production of Manson's work. Soon afterwards, Manson got to know two rather more influential music business people. Beach Boy Dennis Wilson and songwriter/performer/producer Terry Melcher, who was also Doris Day's son, incidentally, — there are theories expressed that 'The Family' killed Sharon Tate by mistake, when they were actually attempting to kill Melcher — and at some point, a song written by Manson, *Never Learn Not To Love*, was recorded by the Beach Boys and the publishing rights to the composition purchased by Denis Wilson. That, of course, is another story . . .

Soon afterwards, Sharon Tate was slain, and Manson and his murderous gang were incarcered, a situation which will hopefully prevail until Manson eventually dies. However, Manson during the early part of his imprisonment, was allowed to make three telephone calls a day, one of which invariably was to Phil Kaufman. As a result of this, Phil made arrangements to release an album of Manson's recordings, presumably in a fund-raising attempt to pay for the latter's defense. It came out in 1970 on a label called Awareness Records, production credit going to 'Phil 12258cal', Kaufman's prison identification number. The evil which permeates this LP is beyond description, from the ghastly photograph of Manson on the front cover to the sleeve note in the form of an interview with Manson, quite obviously a mentally unbalanced person, to the actual songs. This is not a record to enjoy in any way.

Phil Kaufman's luck improved for a while — he met Mick Jagger and became some kind of assistant/tour manager/guide to the Rolling Stones. Phil tells the story of how he and Jagger once walked along Sunset Strip in swimming costumes to go to a bank. Mick Jagger attempted to cash a check, and was asked by the bank teller for identification — too bad he had picked one of the few people in America, and especially in Hollywood, who could not instantly recognize him! Through the Stones, Kaufman met Gram Parsons, a young American singer/songwriter with a deep interest in both rock music and country & western who would eventually make a serious attempt to fuse the two previously mutually exclusive

musical forms. The group he formed to play what became country/rock was the Flying Burrito Brothers, and their tour manager was Phil Kaufman, who dubbed himself the chief of what he called his 'Executive Nanny Service'.

Some time later, Parsons left the Burrito Brothers to embark on a solo career, taking Kaufman with him again as tour manager, and in this period, the two became firm friends, at one point making a pact that if either were to die, the survivor would take the body to a place where both enjoyed going, the Joshua Tree National Monument, a large expanse of land situated directly to the east of Los Angeles, much of which was a desert. During the second half of 1973, Parsons did in fact succumb to a drug overdose, but fulfilling his part of the pact was not easy for Phil Kaufman. Parsons' family, from whom he was virtually estranged, had decided that they wanted the singer buried in his home town, and arrangements were completed for the body to be flown to Louisiana, and it took some ingenuity for Kaufman to recruit a like minded conspirator, to borrow a hearse, and to time his arrival at the airport from which the body was to be shipped to the minute. Explaining that plans had been changed, and that the body was to be flown from a different airport, Kaufman signed a receipt for the coffin (the fact that he signed the name 'Jeremy Nobody' seems to have been overlooked by the original forwarding agent), and drove the hearse towards Joshua Tree. On the way, this being a substantial drive, the pair of bodysnatchers stopped at a bar for some refreshment of the alcoholic type, and also purchased what they thought would be sufficient gasoline to incinerate the coffin and its contents. Arriving at the National Monument, and by now a little the worse for wear after toasting Gram's

memory in a rather intemperate manner, they unloaded the coffin and tried to set it alight. Unfortunately, their advanced state of inebriation made this task rather difficult, and the result was that the local fire brigade was alerted by a local inhabitant, and the fire was extinguished before the body had been totally engulfed by flames.

Curiously, Kaufman was not charged with stealing the body, nor with attempting to burn it. In the absence of a witness to the original pact, it was impossible to prove that anything illegal had taken place, with the exception of Kaufman being fined a certain amount for destroying a coffin which did not belong to him. Should the reader's reaction to this story be one of horror, a short conversation with Phil Kaufman, one of the friendliest and pleasantest people one could ever hope to meet, would surely lead to the impression that his actions involved no evil intent – the fact that he is now the well-respected tour manager for Emmylou Harris and the Hot Band, one of the most famous and successful groups currently active, should underline this impression, while it may be of interest to note that, in order to pay the fine levied by the courts for burning Parsons' coffin, Kaufman organized a benefit concert in his backyard in Van Nuys, California, which was attended by around one hundred people who paid five dollars each entrance, watched music played by Jonathan Richman and the Modern Lovers and by Bobby 'Boris' Pickett and the Crypt-Kickers, and drank specially labeled 'Gram Pilsner' beer.

THE WORST...
and of the best
the worst
of the rest

Considering the trouble in which the Rolling Stones have found themselves during their career of nearly twenty years at the time of writing, they have released an amazingly small number of bad records. A late '60s fixation with Lucifer resulted in *Their Satanic Majesties Request,* pretty definitely the worst LP (both from titular and musical points of view) that they have ever made, while *Sympathy For The Devil* (a musical highpoint of the 1968 *Beggar's Banquet* album) also rates fairly low in the tasty title stakes.

Elsewhere in this volume can be found reference to the infamous *Cocksucker Blues,* and one or two of Decca's dubious repackaging jobs may have left some customers feeling cheated, but probably the only occasion on which the Stones could be accused of a certain cynicism relates to a 1965 EP, *Got Live If You Want It,* which includes a very brief 'track' titled *We Want The Stones,* consisting of the audience chanting the 'title' four times. It would seem that it was quite unnecessary to treat this audience noise as a track, and adorn it with a title — it could have quite easily been attached to the start of the actual first track with nothing lost. Except, of course, the publishing royalties — *We Want The Stones* is credited to 'Nanker-Phelge', the pseudonym which the group used periodically for songwriting exploits. The fact that all the other tracks on the EP bar an equally flimsy effort titled *I'm Alright* were the compositional work of others makes the publishing theory all too credible.

David Bowie has long been the subject of controversy; he once arrived at a large London railway station adorned in what could best be described as Nazi regalia, hardly the smartest piece of personal PR — or was it?

Unfortunately there are several examples of a below par Bowie on disc — before he became a mystical superstar who only emerged into the outside world occasionally (this ploy was highly successful in keeping the Bowie star lustrous despite the quality of some of his records, which barely escape an honorable mention in this book, compared to the high standards Bowie usually sets.

Bowie lived in Beckenham in Kent, and was a fairly normal bisexual would-be rock star, who made quite a number of unsuccessful tracks for several record companies. When he achieved success the companies for whom he had recorded early in his career wasted little time in reissuing his flops, and it is to the credit of the Bowie following that only one of these refried revivals became a hit. This novelty single (the only polite word is novelty) was titled *The Laughing Gnome* and no doubt only succeeded due to its being a complete contrast to the work with which Bowie later succeeded. Doing his finest Anthony Newley impression, Bowie sings/speaks a pathetically stupid composition full of puns of a standard which might turn on a delinquent baby, but is most unlikely to be of interest to anyone else. The real surprise is that Bowie, despite having controlled his own destiny with great success in recent years, appears not to have made attempts to purchase these desperately poor tracks in order to destroy them.

THE ROCK BOTTOM

1. ***The Deal***
Patrick Campbell

2. ***No Charge*** J J Barrie

3. ***Rock Bottom*** Lynsey de Paul and Mike Moran

4. ***Drive Safely, Darling*** Tony Christie

5. ***Ally's Tartan Army*** Andy Cameron

6. ***Too Drunk to Fuck*** Dead Kennedys

7. ***My Ding-a-Ling*** Chuck Berry

8. ***If I Said You Had a Beautiful Body Would You Hold It Against Me?***
Bellamy Brothers

9. ***Jeremy is Innocent*** Rex Barker and the Ricochets

10. ***Nice Legs, Shame About Her Face*** The Monks

11. ***I'm Qualified to Satisfy*** Barry White

12. ***Lick a Smurp for Christmas***
Father Abraphart and the Smurps

13. ***Deck of Cards*** Max Bygraves

14. ***I Remember Elvis Presley*** Danny Mirror

◄ J. J. Barrie

Barry White

30 SINGLES CHART

15. ***Crescendo*** Hazel Gummidge

16. ***Good Grief Christina*** Chicory Tip

17. ***It's Up To You Petula*** Edison Lighthouse

18. ***The Man From Nazareth*** John Paul Joans

19. ***You Need Wheels*** Merton Parkas

20. ***Two Little Boys*** Rolf Harris

21. ***(You're) Having My Baby*** Paul Anka

22. ***Hurry Up Harry*** Sham 69

23. ***One Day at a Time*** Lena Martell

24. ***What's Your Sign, Girl?*** Barry Biggs

25. ***Desiderata*** Les Crane

26. ***Yet to the Neutron Bomb*** The Maleiates

27. ***The Laughing Gnome*** David Bowie

28. ***When a Child Is Born*** Johnny Mathis

29. ***The Sparrow*** The Ramblers

30. ***The Seagull's Name was Nelson*** Peter Bennett

Sham 69

Singles

Crescendo Hazel Gummidge
There is reason to believe that this colorful alias disguises one Adrienne 'Aj' Webber, a promising, if insubstantial folksinger who enjoyed a few good live reviews in the early '70s. This is no more or less than pointless, and the fact that the songwriting credit is to 'd'Abo' leads one to believe that the erstwhile lead singer of the Manfred Mann group was down on his luck at this time.

Never 'Ad Nothin' Angelic Upstarts
A singularly unattractive band from the North East of England indulge in the primal punk thrash, seemily on the subject of a deprived youth who is shot in some urban fracas.

Angelic Upstarts

Silent Night The Dickies
Not dissimilar to the Angelic Upstarts, but is a version of the Christmas carol which has never received such a thoroughly good kicking in all its life. 'Heavenly peace', eh?

Too Drunk To Fuck Dead Kennedys
Ho Ho! What a joke if we make a record with a title they can't say on the radio – and won't it be funny if it gets in the chart, and they can't play it on the chart shows? No.

Now It's Paul McCartney, Stevie Wonder, Alice Cooper, Elton John Clive Baldwin

A 'novelty' record (is there any greater trademark of no quality?) about a man who has been frozen since 1950, and is being updated on the musical scene of the mid-1970s. For some unknown reason, the man continually sings Al Jolson songs, which were of course popular another quarter of a century before he was frozen, and this destroys what little point there was in the whole thing.

Sex and Drugs and Rock'n'Roll Wake Up and Make Love With Me

Patrick Juvet and His Sweet Perversions

Ian Dury's two fine songs to an unpleasantly throbbing disco beat and sung as if by French persons trying to speak English. Colored sleeve too, therefore an expensive joke for somebody, apparently on Michael Zacha, about whom it has been said "Who?"

Yes to The Neutron Bomb The Moderates

The bomb which kills people but leaves buildings intact. Does anyone need to know more?

Another Close Shave Mr John Dowie

This is an EP, and while there are several songs among its six titles, I must confess that the idea of *I Don't Want To Be Your Amputee* is pretty nauseating, and somewhat less than diverting. Good marks, though, for a sleeve note which reads: 'This is a stereo record. If played on mono equipment, it will sound worse than having your head pushed up a dead bear's bum'.

Jeremy is Innocent Rex Barker and the Ricochets

Referring to Jeremy Thorpe's notorious court case concerning his relationship with a homosexual, whose dog was shot by a hired killer, this is aesthetically pointless, and musically confusing, containing as it does the familiar guitar refrain from *Peter Gunn* by Duane Eddy punctuated by a dog impersonator woofing and a chorus chanting incessantly 'Jeremy Jeremy'. About as funny as a hysterectomy.

The Kinshasa Fight Parts One and Two

Gung Ho

A Swedish record, presumably concerning a boxing match between Muhammad Ali and George Foreman which took place in Zaire. This has the doubtful virtue of being incomprehensible, save for the odd word penetrating the dense backing.

Patrick Juvet

Deep Purple

Deep Purple was an impressive heavy metal band, arguably achieving even greater fame following their demise than they did during their active career. Erstwhile Purple members later formed or joined bands like Whitesnake, Rainbow and Gillan, and hardly a month passes without some suggestion that a Deep Purple reunion is being considered. This could present several problems, not least the fact that both Ian Gillan, and his successor as Purple vocalist David Coverdale, both have their devotees.

One aspect of the group's career which is often forgotten concerns their early days —while Purple heroes Ritchie Blackmore, Jon Lord and Ian Price were in the band more or less from its inception, the arrival of Ian Gillan and Roger Glover, who completed the Mark Two' line up of the group generally considered to be its most effective, did not occur until several

years later. Before they were recruited, Purple released a number of records with varying degrees of success, and possibly the most unpleasant of the tracks recorded during this period was a disastrous version of the Neil Diamond pseudo-epic, *Kentucky Woman,* which appeared on an album with the pretentious title *The Book Of Taliesyn,* the significance of which, it seems, has never intrigued anyone writing about the group enough to inquire as to its origin. The same album, by the way, also includes Purple's version of the tender Lennon-McCartney song, *We Can Work It Out,* which, like *Kentucky Woman,* is performed in an absurdly bombastic manner by four fifths of the group, the exception being mad axeman Blackmore, who plays some blood curdling lines as though pretending that he's not really a member of the band – good on him!

Beach Boys

The lengthy career of the Beach Boys (who played their first gig on New Year's Eve, 1961, when most members of the group were still at school) has been punctuated with problems of various types. Dennis Wilson's involvement with psychopath of the century Charles Manson, Mike Love's lengthy and continuing involvement with Transcendental Mediation ("I've been learning how to to fly," he told one writer. "We do it in this padded room, and it's just incredible to see all these people flying around like birds" – no doubt with brains to match!), numerous quarrels with record companies, and concerts being cancelled at a few days notice following poor advance ticket sales are just a few of the traumas which have afflicted the 'Kings of Surf Music', most of whom, it should be note, have a strong aversion to the actual sport of surfing.

There have been dozens of poor Beach Boys tracks released during their twenty years of making records, but perhaps two of the worst occurred relatively recently, perhaps a sad reflection of the group's fall from prominence as they grew older – how many 'boys' are there who are almost completely bald? A 1977 album titled *The Beach Boys Love You* was apparently designed as a 'comeback' for the one genious in the band, the oldest of the three Wilson brothers, Brian.

Two or three cuts on the album seemed to indicate that the wayward genius was on the mend, although many others cast serious doubts on any possible recovery, in particular something called *Ding Dang*, whose composer credit lists Brian Wilson and Roger McGuinn, erstwhile leader of another famous group, the Byrds. It is difficult to believe that it took two people to write a song whose entire lyrical content, apart from a number of random 'dings' and 'dangs' consists of the following lines:

> I love a girl,
> I love her so madly.
> I treat her fine but she treats me so badly.

The song's greatest virtue is that it lasts no longer than fifty-seven seconds, but surely, who could be expected to believe in some miraculous recovery for the oldest Wilson when a piece of kindergarten poetry is incuded on his 'comeback'?

But this ranks as a masterpiece compared to a track on another 'comeback' LP, this time supposedly for the group as a whole rather then just Brian. The particularly guilty party on this occasion was lead vocalist Mike Love who wrote a song with so little backbone that it induces nausea in the writer to merely type the song's title – *Sumahama*. This nugget, lasting nearly four and a half minutes, is sung in a ridiculously affected voice, and even contains several portions sung in Japanese. How appropriate for the group often considered as the epitomé of the All American Band.

THE WORST...

Mention is made elsewhere of the execrable *Having Fun With Elvis On Stage* LP, but regrettably, this was only a part of the Presley Rock Bottom catalog – during his lifetime the fact that Elvis was in decline was perfectly plain to anyone who had heard his initial and ultimately exciting performances, although a solid core of Presleyophiles was always on hand to purchase the latest outrage released with the magic name on the sleeve. An interesting fact which emerged some time after Presley's 1977 death was that until the release of a compilation titled *Elvis Presley Sings Leiber and Stoller,* a fine LP which pictured Presley and the two songwriters on its sleeve, there had never been a Presley LP sleeve containing a picture of anyone other than Elvis.

To return to our theme, after drugs and dissipation had claimed Elvis, his record company bit their collective lip for some time before assembling a package which they felt would do justice to Presley's memory (or, as the more cynically inclined might say, would be sufficient to prise a lot of money out of the pockets of Presley fans), the eventual result being an eight LP boxed set with accompanying booklet, which sold for a princely $75. The theory was that if a percentage of the included material were to be previously unreleased, a financial bonanza could be achieved with little effort, and it has to be admitted that this theory held water, as the limited edition' of fifty thousand or more sets sold out at some speed.

When the devout arrived home after making this somewhat large investment, there were no doubt a number of delighted people among them. However, the less committed might have been a little surprised to discover that each of the eight albums was contained in a very flimsy thin cardboard wrapper (admittedly containing a full color picture of Elvis) and that no inner sleeve of polythene or even paper had been provided to afford the extra protection which a normal album needs. A good deal of the recorded material was not new at all – two and half LPs, in fact – while two other complete discs were filled with alternate takes of songs recorded either for films or in live performance in Las Vegas. The term 'alternate take' may sound intriguing, but on the basis of what is heard here, it simply means incomplete or inferior recordings of songs released in a superior form elsewhere. Yet another whole LP plus one side of another are taken up with more live recordings – if these versions had been so good, one wonders why they were not used in place of versions of the songs that were released.

Which leaves four sides of Elvis doing something entirely new, out of a total of sixteen sides. In fairness, three of the sides are completely new, and although once again these are live recordings, they were made at interesting points during Elvis' early career, and as such are of value both intrinsically and musically. The remaining half an album is a recording of Elvis delivering a somewhat unrevealing monolog about himself, which lasts for a generous thirteen minutes and forty one seconds. Mention of durations brings up another peeve – there can have been little or no origination cost in preparing this pile of generally substandard recordings for release, although some of the recordings needed studio treatment to bring them up to a level which was just acceptable in sound quality. The total time of the complete eight LP set amounts to one minute over four hours, an average per disc of a few seconds more than thirty minutes. As each of the records cost somewhat more than $9 to purchase, it could hardly be claimed that the set offered value for money, especially as it contained only three sides (approximately forty five minutes) of genuinely new music by Presley. Three quarters of an hour for seventy-five bucks? No doubt there will be a follow up album of similar material released before long . . .

Angie(?) and Pete Townshend

As a group, The Who have always produced music to which there could be little objection. As their career progressed, individual group members released solo albums, and these have generally been little better than interesting, a notable exception being Pete Townshend's excellent *Empty Glass* album released in 1980. However, Townshend's first solo effort, released in 1972, was titled *Who Came First,* and was considerably disturbing to those unaware that the album's commercial release was the result of substantial sales of a 'devotional' album released privately and intended as purely of interest to those who shared Townshend's interest in the teachings of the Indian 'guru', Meher Baba. This accounts for the inclusion of Baba's favorite song, made famous by Jim Reeves, *There's A Heartache Following Me,* which Townshend performs exactly like Reeves, plus items performed by fellow Baba disciples Ronnie Lane and Billy Nicholls. There are also several rather good songs included, *Pure And Easy, Let's See Action* and *Sheraton Gibson,* for instance, but overall the unwary buyer could be somewhat discontented by the purchase of this album.

THE ROCK BOTTOM

1. *A Blow For Me, A Toot For You*
   Fred Wesley and the Horny Horns

2. *The Jesus of Cool* Nick Lowe

3. *The Ventures Play the Classics*

4. *Come Again* Derek and Clive

5. *Rumours* Fleetwood Mac

6. *Max* The Rumour

7. *Concerto for Group and Orchestra*
   Deep Purple and the Royal Philharmonic Orchestra

8. *Live and Sleazy* The Village People

9. *Consequences* Creme and Godley

10. *Contractual Obligation Album* Monty Python

11. *The Six Wives of Henry VIII* Rick Wakeman

12. *You Can Tune a Piano,
    But You Can't Tuna Fish*
    R E O Speedwagon

13. *New Hope for the Wretched* Plasmatics

14. *Derek and Clive Live*
    Peter Cook and Dudley Moore

15. *Holly Days* Denny Laine

16. *100 Golden Greats* Max Bygraves

17. *Neil Reid* Neil Reid

18. *Flogging a Dead Horse* Sex Pistols

19. *A Christmas Together*
    John Denver and the Muppets

20. *Sid Sings* Sid Vicious

20 ALBUMS CHART

Notes

1. Ex-James Brown backing musicians aim at both sex and drugs markets.
2. What you need is a clip round the ear with a thunderbolt or two.
3. And lose!
4. The follow up to 14—but it's more a threat than an invitation.
5. & 6. The first sold about ten million, the second about ten thousand. There's a lesson there somewhere.
7. Spot the odd one out.
8. Dead and smelly.
9. A triple album which cost several million pounds and sold several hundred copies.
10. One of the more accurate titles on any album.

11. To be performed on ice in a zoo.
12. You can hit a record, but you can't record a hit.
13. No hope for the tasteful.
14. What's the worst job you ever had? Listening to this LP.
15. Buddy Holly buried.
16. Every masochist should have one.
17. Child prodigy, OK?
18. See 10.
19. Christmas, the Muppets and John Denver—what a resistable combination.
20. Recorded posthumously—at least, that's what it sounds like.

Nick Lowe

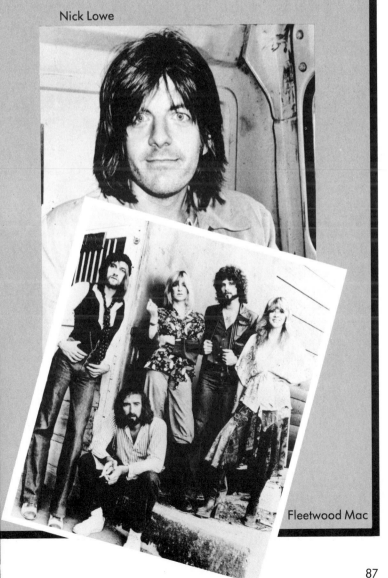

Fleetwood Mac

Village People

Rick Wakeman

THE WORST...

Albums

Chicago at Carnegie Hall
As a group, Chicago certainly had a substantial following, and several of their recordings might be loosely termed classics. One virtue which they seemed to never appreciate, however, was brevity — their first three releases were double album sets, but with this fourth release, the unsuspecting listener got not only a live set, but a quadruple live set. The case rests . . .

The Ventures Play The Classics
While in Britain Cliff Richard's old backing group the Shadows are recognized as the pioneers of the electric guitar, at least in terms of bringing it to public recognition, this mantle was adopted in America by the Ventures. Nevertheless, there was little excuse for this waste of time and vinyl — can there be anyone who would wish to hear *Jesu Joy Of Man's Desiring* played to a rocking beat by a guitarist who seemed to be trying to beat the clock?

Roddy Roddy Llewellyn
When they define the word 'bad' in dictionaries, some of the definitions are words like 'defective', 'worthless' and 'putrid'. Certainly, 'bad' seems an appropriate description of this LP, which is described elsewhere, but it should not be thought that Roddy is alone in having accepted the offer to make an album — and to be paid for it! Among other opportunists who have made similar mistakes (if it's a mistake to be paid well for doing something rather badly for which you haven't been trained) are golfers (Gary Player among others), dozens of soccer players and other assorted sportspeople, Senator Sam, Quentin Crisp — the list is not only endless, it grows more endless with each passing day.

Chipmunk Punk The Chipmunks
In 1958, an American of Armenian extraction named Ross Bagdasarian, who had enjoyed some good fortune as a songwriter, hit upon the idea of recording

Chicago

a track at half speed and making it into a record which played at normal speed. His first attempt, *Witch Doctor*, which was released under his professional name of David Seville, became a million seller, and encouraged by this, Bagdasarian persisted with the idea, the result being an entirely mythical group known as the Chipmunks (because the resulting voices sounded, it was claimed, like Chipmunks speaking).

The Chipmunk concept was too good a moneymaker to throw away simply because its originator had died – in 1980, some years after punk rock had effectively curled up and died (at least in a commercial sense), came this loathsome album. Of its nine tracks, no less than three were originally recorded by Los Angeles overnight sensations The Knack.

The Bill Black Combo Plays Chuck Berry

On the face of it, an interesting concept. Berry is well known, as the writer of numerous rock 'n' roll classics, and Bill Black was the bass player in Elvis Presley's original backing group, later to make several hits with his own band, after leaving Presley's employ. There is a small drawback, however, which does not become apparent until the record is actually played – the melody of Chuck Berry songs (or at least the vast majority of them) is contained in the vocal, and instrumentally, what remains is little short of supremely tedious. Surprisingly, the same applies to the work of the Beach Boys, who released an album of their own backing tracks with no vocals under the title *Stack-o-Tracks*. Just how meaningless classic songs can sound without their vocals becomes apparent very quickly – although not quickly enough for those who have paid money for such artefacts.

Puttin' On The Style Lonnie Donegan

The most successful British solo artist before Cliff Richard, with thirty hit records between 1956 and 1962, Donegan was belatedly recognized as the inspiration behind an army of later British stars, who decided that they would get together to help him make a kind of tribute album in the late 1970s. Rory Gallagher, Leo Sayer, Ringo Starr, Elton John and a lot more besides were involved, as Lonnie re-recorded a selection of his old hits. And not one sounded ten per cent as good as the scratchy originals. How could this be? One explanation was that by 1977, Lonnie was far from destitute, but in poor health, and thus was not working because he needed to, as had been the case twenty years previously. Moral: let your heroes grow old gracefully; don't try to help them live their pasts.

Lonnie Donegan

The Wit and Wisdom of Ronald Regan

Dealt with elsewhere, this is an entirely silent record. An elaborate joke, certainly, but at considerable expense to anyone who wasn't aware in advance of how warped was the sense of humor of the person who dreamt it up. And wasn't there a crisis not so long ago when the world was short of vinyl? This could hardly have helped ...

A Christmas Together
John Denver and the Muppets

Oddly enough, this book contains few references to Christmas or the Muppets and only one other to John Denver. What an awesome trio to bring together on one LP. There's little future in describing this record, as must be obvious, save to note that in terms of fine musicians playing, it is almost second to none, including several members of Elvis Presley's final band, Hal Blaine, the ultimate session drummer, Jim Horn (ditto for saxophone) and several other highly familiar names. One must presume that they were doing it for the money (and why not?), because they don't have a scale low enough to record this album's musical qualities.

THE WORST...

Holly Days Denny Laine
On the face of it, there's not much wrong with covering a clutch of Buddy Holly songs and packaging them together under a title like *Holly Days*. But when you seem to miss the point of a classic song like *It's So Easy*, removing almost every vestige of life from it, something seems to have gone sadly amiss.

Suburban Studs

Denny Laine

Slam Suburban Studs
The reason why punk rock achieved such a gruesome reputation in its early days was not so much to do with an album like this, but after the good points about punk had been identified and assimilated, bandwagon jumpers like this completely uninspired quartet were the inspiration for every detrimental comment made about punk rockers. The track listing tells all, with poetic titles like *I Hate School, Bondage, Necro, Razor Blades, Two Victims* and *Throbbing Lust*. If you see this record in a shop, take care not to touch it, as a dearth of inspiration is highly contagious, but the obligatory health warning seems to have been left off the sleeve.

Phil Spector

Although it's obviously a subject for debate, the name which would probably be mentioned most often when the subject of record producers is mooted is that of Phil Spector, the diminutive American who became a superstar as a result of his work with several artists who themselves were largely anonymous, operating as pawns in the hitmaking process which Spector mastered during the first half of the 1960s (although he later lost his golden touch). Even so, there was one aspect of his hitmaking technique which was at least slightly suspect, and related to the B sides of many of his hits, which often comprised extraordinarily sloppy instrumentals. Although it was quite obvious to anyone who thought about this for longer than a second that neither the Ronettes nor the Crystals (both all girl groups) were likely to be as adept instrumentally as they were vocally, these B sides were always credited to the same artist as the A side. Additionally, many of these B sides were given cryptic titles, often referring to Spector's relations, associates or even to the musicians who were presumably playing on these bizarre songs, which were without exception almost unlistenable and had every appearance of being thrown

The Ronettes

together at something approaching the speed of light. Thus, the B side of Bob B. Soxx's *Zip-A-Dee-Doo-Dah* is *Flip and Nitty,* presumed to refer to Spector himself and his arranger Jack Nitzsche, while *Dr Kaplan's Office,* the B side to the follow up by Bob B. Soxx, is presumed to relate to sazophonist Artie Kaplan. The Crystals' *Then He Kissed Me* is backed by something titled *Brother Julius,* who was probably marimba player Julius Wechter, while *Be My Baby* by the Ronettes is partnered by *Tedesco and Pitman,* who were both guitar players in the Spector Wall Of Sound, Tommy Tedesco and Bill Pitman.

Spector has rarely been interviewed, but the explanation usually given when inquiries are made about these strange and almost unplayable tracks is that it was Spector's unswerving intention that all attention must be focused on the A side, which actually featured genuine artists. This, of course, is either a piece of brilliant thinking (from Spector's own point of view) or an outrage (from the point of view of those who buy a double sided disc, only to find that one side is worthless). Why, one wonders, did Spector not take the idea to its logical conclusion and release single sided records at half the price, or even press the song on both sides of the record?

The name of Bob Dylan is one well esteemed throughout the civilized world, and records by the man are greatly prized – you're unlikely to find many rock critics over the age of thirty with a less than complete collection of Dylan's authorized releases, along with at least a few bootlegs. However, even before the comparatively recent religious experience which has made Dylan's work anathema to the more insensitive of his admirers, his career encountered a few hiccups during the early 1970s.

The first of these occurred in 1970 itself, when the artist, who by this time was able to instruct his record company as to which of his records they should release, supplied them with a strange double album titled *Self Portrait,* which met with a decidedly hostile response from critics and public alike. The reasons behind this bizarre collection of partially live recordings of familiar self-written epics, partially cover versions of highly unlikely songs, and a few new things, have never been successfulluy explained, and it wasn't long – four months, in fact – before a brand new Dylan LP, with the promising title of *New Morning* giving it all the hallmarks of a fresh start, restored the status quo. Everything was fine for some time, until David Geffen, head of the newly formed Asylum record label, was smart enough to perceive that Dylan's relationship with CBS/Columbia, for whom he had exclusively recorded since his debut in early 1962, was the subject of some dissatisfaction from the artist's point of view.

Perhaps somewhat surprisingly,

Bob Dylan

there are numerous possibilities to be considered when deciding what could truly be termed the worst of the Beatles. Elsewhere in this book can be found mention of the infamous 'butcher cover' and the silent *Nutopian National Anthem* recorded (or not) by John Lennon. Other candidates should perhaps be a brace of Paul McCartney singles released during the early '70s, *Mary Had A Little Lamb* (yes, the nursery rhyme) and the unnecessarily inflammatory *Give Ireland Back To The Irish* an ill-advised comment on the unpleasantness which has been destroying said island for far too many years. Then there's the series of unlistenable albums made by John Lennon and Yoko Ono, *Two Virgins*, which featured a front sleeve photograph of the totally naked pair making no attempt at all to disguise or hide their sexual organs, the even more tedious *Unfinished Music No. 2*, which was a continuation of the sound concept of its predecessor, but with a sleeve showing Yoko in hospital after a miscarriage, and the last in the series, *The Wedding Album*, which quite unintentionally caused great hilarity when it was reviewed by a London music paper journalist who has since graduated to the heavier end of Fleet Street. This unfortunate scribe was sent an advance copy of the record, in the form of two single sided discs. Sadly, he didn't realize that some record companies distribute test pressings in this form, and reviewed the album as though it was a double LP, commenting that he preferred the two sides which contained an electronic hum which lasted for around twenty minutes in each case . . .

The celebrated 'double white' LP (which was actually titled *The Beatles*) also included at least one exceptionally tiresome track, *Revolution No. 9*, which would tax the patience of a saint, while Ringo Starr's first solo album, *Sentimental Journey*, consisted of the drummer singing a series of standards like *Bye Bye Blackbird* and *Stardust* in a less than inspired manner. His excuse, that he made the album for his mother, was still hardly compensation for anyone unfortunate enough to buy the record, while the same could be said of the majority of George Harrison's solo efforts from the 1973 LP, *Living In The Material World*, onwards. But perhaps the prime candidate for the Rock Bottom award must be the one track on the otherwise near perfect *Sargeant Pepper* LP which was also principally the work of George Harrison. *Within You, Without You* is its title, and it reflects Harrison's continuing fixation with Indian music. The fact that it concludes with laughter may be considered as a reflection of the way Lennon and McCartney felt about the track — that with a bit of luck, their laughter might convince the listener that it was intended as a joke. In truth, there is very little about the track which could be classified as a laughing matter.

In 1973, Geffen apparently made Dylan the legendary 'offer he couldn't refuse', and for the space of time it takes to make two albums, Dylan was away from CBS. Letting a major artist go without a fight would be less than creditable, and CBS tried very hard to appease their unhappy megastar. But all to no avail – Dylan refused to contemplate re-signing, so CBS applied the somewhat unsubtle pressure of releasing a hotch potch of mostly very dubious material, some of it out-takes from that earlier *Self Portrait* album, and nearly all of it fairly unpleasant, both aesthetically, and more to the point, musically. The LP on which this nadir of recordings was collected was simply titled *Dylan*, was packaged in an unattractive sleeve, and contained no details other than the track listing. Needless to say, the album was not a success, and it wasn't long before Dylan returned to CBS, 'encouraged', so rumor has it, by the promise of further albums of junk which remained in the possession of CBS. Even so, Dylan reputedly had the last laugh – while renegotiating his contract, he included the stipulation that the rights to all the material he had recorded for CBS should revert to himself after the elapse of a certain number of years.

THE WORST...

By way of a postcript to this review of The Worst, there is a rather weak standing joke in record company marketing departments that concerns the album that ships and returns platinum. The meaning of this doggerel is that sufficient advance sales of a record are made for it to be certified gold on the basis of sales on the day of release, while some time later, the accountants discover that unsold returned copies have miraculously exceeded the number shipped out of the factory. Impossible, you may say – but you are a disbeliever...

The year is 1968, and so called 'underground' music is about to become the happening thing. Several record companies have made bargain purchases of groups from fashionable parts of America, in particular San Francisco, and seem to be reaping the benefits. It seems that only one major record label, Capitol Records, have not become involved in the horse trading, but it has finally been decreed that they will enter the market. It seems that this slow approach has paid off – the first wave of genuinely talented bands have signed elsewhere, and at this point in time, a good deal of rubbish is being offered a lot of money by talent scouts who reckon that geography is of far greater importance than talent. Anyone walking around San Francisco with long hair can seemingly become a recording artist (and the proof was in the bargain bins for some years afterwards).

Capitol, having started late in the game, can afford to be choosy – or rather, they can't afford to be choosy, because they are fortunate enough to sign three of the best bands available – Quicksilver Messenger Service, The Band (Bob Dylan's erstwhile backing group) and the Steve Miller Band – all of whom will eventually sell many millions of records and presumably make a good deal of money for the company. However, the acquisition of these acts involves larger sums of money than have ever been paid to any recording artist previously, which leaves Capitol with the problem of tiding over budgetary problems until such time as the new signings recoup their investments. Capitol also signs other acts during this period, few, if any, of whom will become successful, and one of whom is of particular relevance to the subject under discussion.

Hippie groups is where it is at in 1968, and when the chance comes to sign an unknown seven piece band called The Wind In The Willows, it is swiftly taken. A bearded hippy with wire-rim glasses, one with a moustache and glasses, another one with a beard and a cosmic stare and a couple of girls are included in this line up, plus someone called Freddy, whose credit on the group's LP sleeve is as 'spiritual advisor' – what more could be asked for? In retrospect, the answer that screams out is 'talent', but as we've already discussed, that was low on the list of priorities in 1968 – image was everything. The album is released, and due to the fact that the entire record industry is overtaken with friendly optimism, it ships a substantial number of copies. Then comes bad news – several months later, retailers are returning them in droves, to the point where the returns eventually exceed sales, a mind- and logic-bending statistic. The answer was discovered by a Capitol executive, who inspected some of the returns and found, much to his surprise, that among them were several hundred promotional copies of the album – putting two and two together, it became clear that not only had shops sold virtually zero copies, but the vast majority of reviewers had also sold or exchanged their review copies, and these had somehow been included among the returns. In accounting terms, this had the effect of producing sales of a minus quantity, which must have taken a highly-developed sense of humor to swallow gracefully.

All this might be considered an insignificant curio, were it not for the fact that among the members of The Wind In The Willows was a young girl credited on the album sleeve with vocals, tamboura, tambourine and finger cymbals. Her name? Deborah Harry, although the sleeve picture of the lady the world now knows as Blondie gives little away, as in 1968, Debbie had not yet resorted to peroxide to produce the effect which has become her trademark more than twelve years later. The record company was not slow to reissue the album after Blondie became famous, although one small change was made to the sleeve artwork, which now reads: 'The Wind In The Willows featuring Debbie Harry'. The greatest heroes always have the heaviest crosses to bear.

THE ROCK BOTTOM 20 LP SLEEVES

1. **Down Two, Then Left** Boz Scaggs
2. **Just Family** Dee Dee Bridgewater
3. **Touch**
4. **Shrink**
5. **The Ballad of Lucy Jordan**
   Dr Hook and the Medicine Show
6. **The Force** Real Thing
7. **Reality Effect** The Tourists
8. **After the Rain** Muddy Waters
9. **Loonee Tunes** Bad Manners
10. **Futuristic Dragon** T Rex
11. **Hot Rods** Rod Stewart
12. **Greatest Hits Volume II** Cockney Rejects
13. **Act Like Nothing's Wrong** Al Kooper
14. **Child is Father to the Man**
    Blood, Sweat and Tears
15. **Flogging a Dead Horse** The Sex Pistols
16. **Jumpin' the Gunne** Jo Jo Gunne
17. **Lovedrive** The Scorpions
18. **Two Virgins** John Lennon/Yoko Ono
19. **Best of Pop Sounds** The Ventures
20. **Below the Belt** Boxer

RECORD SLEEVE SLEAZE – cover art to forget

It's never been terribly clear

just what is so funny about a nun – aside from various aspects of schoolboy humor, there doesn't appear to be much surrounding these devout ladies which can produce any emotion other than respect. However, rock musicians seem to feel that a picture of a nun on their record sleeves, especially a nun doing things which nuns are generally not presumed to do very often, if at all, gives their records some odd kind of distinction. Mick Farren, now a respected rock writer in New York, used to front a somewhat desperate group known as The Deviants, one of whose LPs sported a sleeve which showed a decidedly lascivious nun enjoying a somewhat phallic lollipop. It hardly needs to be said that this appears to have little or nothing to do with the record inside . . . At least the Deviants didn't title their record *Bad Habits*, a temptation two other groups were unable to resist when decorating their LP covers with a nun. One of these, a band calling themselves Headstone (and that name sounds at least a little suspect) found themselves a nun wearing lipstick and smoking a cigarette in the manner of a very poor man's Lauren Bacall, but as the group vanished into obscurity shortly after the release of their one LP, one must charitably assume that the idea of the sleeve was an attempt to draw attention to their record, whose content was presumably deemed too weak to achieve a similar effect on its own merits.

Neither The Deviants nor Headstone ever became famous (although the former might make a justifiable claim that they became somewhat notorious), but a third 'nun' sleeve graced an album made by two musicians whose work has probably been heard by a substantial number of record buyers. During the early '70s, Richard Hudson and John Ford were members of The Strawbs, a folk/rock group whose major claim

Mick Farren of the Devients

Hudson (R) and Ford (2nd L) of The Strawbs

to fame was an unlikely pseudo-protest song entitled *Part Of The Union*. While it might be felt that ridiculing Trade Unions was a possibly funny and undoubtedly brave enterprise, it might not be too far from the truth to suggest that the current state of siege in which Britain finds itself could partially have resulted from such dubious attempts at humor, especially as the record became the group's biggest hit, entering the top three of the chart at the start of 1973 (the year, you may recall which ended with the three day week).

After leaving the Strawbs, Hudson and Ford achieved three smaller hits under their own name in the first half of the decade, before apparently vanishing for some time. They did not re-emerge in any substantial way until 1979, when they scored a top twenty hit with the somewhat cruel *Nice Legs, Shame About The Face*, undoubtedly one of the most male chauvinist singles of all time, when they called themselves The Monks. Their sole LP, called *Bad Habits* again, showed what in truth must be termed the best looking nun of the three under review here, although once again the cigarette hanging from the corner of her mouth, not to mention the fact that she seems to be adjusting her suspender belt, leads one to believe that the lady is more interested in deviation than devotion – which of course brings this discussion full circle . . .

RECORD SLEEVE SLEAZE

Scorpions – Lovedrive (courtesy E.M.I. Records)

The Scorpions were never known as the most subtle of bands, but on this, their first hit album in Britain, things were taken to ridiculous extremes. Where's the fun in discovering bubblegum (or perhaps something even more appalling) on the nice lady's right bosom? What makes the whole thing even more bizarre is that the gentleman with the handful of goo is not only a model, but at other times has worked as a cook at top London music theater, The Venue – think about that when you order a meal!

Jo Jo Gunne was a very promising band during the mid-1970's, but the sleeve which adorned (the phrase is used in its loosest sense) the album

Jumpin' the Gunne can have done little for the average potential punter leafing through the browser. The outside of the LP depicts the four band members sitting in a large bed together, all apparently aghast at the sight of a plumpish human leg hovering near the ceiling. However, on folding our the cover the can appreciate the boys' jaw droop a little more. Suffice to say, it reveals the horizontal 'flying' figure of a nude female so generous in proportion that if she crash landed, thousands would suffer in the fall out. To ram the point home a small pig looks on. A repetition of the 'motif' on the inside is even more hideous; the credits are inscribed on the contours of the same anonymous lady, like a diagram explaining cuts of meat in a butcher's shop.

Boz Scaggs is without doubt one of the nicest people walking about in the maelstrom with the deceptively harmless title of rock music. It took Boz several years of trying before he hit upon a blend of music which met with the commercial success his fans had always known couldn't be far away. The breakthrough LP was titled *Silk Degrees*, and spawned a slew of hit singles back in 1976, but if the quality of an album sleeve could have anything to do with the record's sale potential, the absurd *Down Two Then Left*, which was in fact the follow up LP to *Silk Degrees*, might have put Boz even further back than before he broke the hit barrier. It pictures Boz striding out from a doorway, leaving behind three life-size ice effigies melting rapidly in the shadows. What? Cooler than ice? More meaningless than a puddle on the sidewalk?

THE DESERVEDLY OBSCURE BAND

Mom's Apple Pie caused a minor tremor in the world of retailers and other honest folk with the cover of their first album. It depicted 'mom' clutching a pie with one slice removed and hidden among the apples was a drawing of a vagina. After appropriate outrage the missing slice was replaced, the pie was adorned with barbed wire and 'mom' was provided with tears in her eyes!

BECOMING PREGNANT IS UNDOUBTEDLY

a source of great joy to the female sex, at least in most cases. However, it is sometimes difficult for some ladies to comprehend that their joy is not something to be shared by the public at large. Whether or not the extremely expectant lady pictured on this LP sleeve is in fact Dee Dee Bridgewater is difficult to ascertain — however, it would appear that the lady posing behind her stomach in the middle of the desert (albeit bathed in the optimistic light of early morning), was taking a considerable risk in travelling so far from civilization when the arrival of her offspring was so obviously imminent.

Dee Dee Bridgewater

AND THEN THERE'S RODDY LLEWELLYN, FOR MANY YEARS

the confidant of Princess Margaret, sister of the Queen Elizabeth II. Llewellyn's occupation lay in the field of horticulture, but, alas, he was only human, and when it was suggested to him that he make an album singing romantic ballads, his ego became sufficiently massaged for him to agree. The resulting album is frankly awful – whatever other talents Llewllyn may possess, the ability to sing is conspicuous by its absence. In a 'handwritten' note on the sleeve, Roddy writes: "Like lots of other people I have always wanted to make a record, and I feel very fortunate to have now done this. We all had a lot of fun recording the album – hope you enjoy it too!". It would hardly be truthful to indicate that the majority of those few who bought the record can have experienced the emotion of enjoyment – the album has now become an in demand kitsch collector's item, and those close relations (presumably) who are awaiting a follow-up look destined for a rather lengthy wait . . .

Roddy Llewellyn – Roddy (courtesy Phonogram)

Dr. Hook and the Medicine Show are a well known group nowadays, but their early records for CBS, with the notable exception of *Sylvia's Mother*, were not good sellers although they were in no way sub-standard, and in fact are considered by many experts to be infinitely superior to the sentimental drivel which later made them famous. The sleeve to the album, *The Ballad of Lucy Jordan* did the group few favors, as its title failed to accurately reflect that this was a collection of the group's finest performances during the early part of their career. More serious, though, is the ghastly cover art – the front of the sleeve is little short of unnecessarily grotesque, – the group's name tattoed onto a pimples-and-all close up of a hairy chest – while the rear, with its absurd collection of surgical appliances, is presumably an attempt, by someone who obviously failed to realize that the group's name was not to be taken seriously, at reflecting the 'medicine' element. As a side issue, it may be of interest to learn that the same art director perpetrated at least one other

Dr Hook

atrocity during his career: a budget priced reissue of the second LP by The Byrds, a group who made many records and whose personnel frequently changed, featured a picture of the wrong line up of the group as related to the record in question – not only was there the wrong number of Byrds, but the group pictured on the sleeve functioned some seven years after the group which recorded the album.

The Sex Pistols may actually have had little to do with the sleeve to their *Greatest Hits* LP, amusingly titled *Flogging A Dead Horse*. The front, featuring the lady in hot pants camping it up with the classic hand-behind-the-head, pin-up pose, and clutching two rather runny looking ice creams to her breast, is gross in a subtle sort of way. There doesn't seem to be anything even faintly subtle about the doggy do-do on the reverse of the sleeve. As far as poor old Sid Vicious goes, his pose on the front of the truly horrendous *Sid Sings* LP was just one further example of the unfortunate boy who never grew up. Unlike Peter Pan, though, Sid became a lost boy with smack and a spike . . .

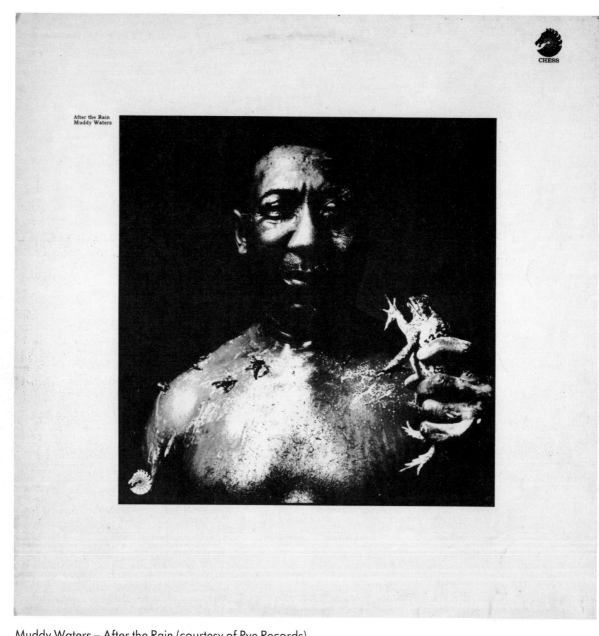

Muddy Waters – After the Rain (courtesy of Pye Records)

Quite what it is that makes this sleeve so disturbing cannot really be explained, but it certainly induces a cringe. Like so many of the acts whose records are featured here, the band have fortunately disappeared. That's not true at all of Muddy Waters, of course, but soon after he made the LP whose sleeve is pictured here, he did little recording for some years.

It always seemed that *Star Wars* was a particularly pleasant film in terms of the lack of unnecessary sex etc., which made it doubly unfortunate when black British group The Real Thing (their name alone must give rise to some doubts – the real what thing?) released a single which was undeniably suggested by *Star Wars*, *Can You Feel The Force?* and scored a big hit. As a result, an album by the group was also titled after the 45 – as can plainly be seen here, the sleeve designer obviously possessed a little less imagination and sensitivity than an average inercontinental ballistic missile.

The Real Thing – Can You Feel The Force (courtesy P.R.T.)

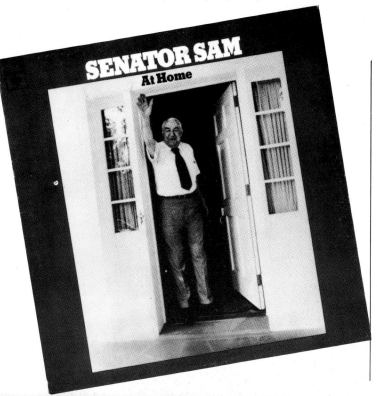

Senator Sam – At Home (courtesy Columbia Records)

OCCASIONALLY, RECORD COMPANIES

get what they consider to be bright ideas, into which category fall albums by soccer players, other types of sportsmen and famous personalities, etc. Two particularly dreadful examples of this type of inspiration immediately stick out, the earlier being by an American politician, Senator Sam Ervin, who recorded Senator Sam At Home during 1973, when he was seventy seven years old. Quite why this respected and respectable man decided to open himself up to the derision which greeted the release of the record is not clear – however, it contains several recitations by the Senator of poetry and prose, which are acceptable if the listener has a strong stomach and a well cultivated sense of the absurd, plus some positively unspeakable singing, the worst example being a rendition of Simon and Garfunkel's Bridge Over Troubled Water. It is conceivable that by now the Senator is resting in peace – let us earnestly hope that he is not disturbed by the sound of his own voice, as many of those still on this mortal coil have been . . .

The Cockney Rejects are mentioned elsewhere in this volume in the gross context, but here's a little visual example of their cheery cock sparrer etc., appeal. This, by the way, is possibly as inaccurate as any record ever released, and the 'music' by this quartet of hooligans might easily be a contributory factor in the escalating violence which makes a pop concert of the '80s a major health hazard much of the time. Rock off, boys – the only thing you'd be good for is sub-human vivisection.

Cockney Rejects – Greatest Hits Vol 2 (courtesy E.M.I. Records)

RECORD SLEEVE SLEAZE

T. Rex – Futuristic Dragon (courtesy E.M.I. Records)

During his highly successful career, Marc Bolan was accused of many things, pretention being just one vice among many. Before his unfortunate and untimely death in a motor accident, Bolan was beginning to fade from the limelight, possibly due to items like this sleeve to the final officially released album before he died. The look on the caricature Bolan's face would be enough to bring tears of laughter, were it not for the fact that his death was so tragic.

There really isn't anything much to say about the sleeve for yet another repackage of ex-grave digger Rod Stewart's early recordings, called, would you believe, *Hot Rods*. It's almost a surprise it didn't boast a picture of a stock car of some sort . . . Printed in second hand day glo color, Mr Stewart is seen romping suggestively on the front cover with an erect fluorescent tube in his hands. Yawn.

Rod Stewart

The Tourists were a highly promising and very interesting group, whose demise during the early part of 1981 was one of the more unfortunate occurrences of that period. However, considering what the band allowed to pass for the cover of their second LP, *Reality Effect*, it might be thought that this was a group with a death wish. Striking? Certainly. Meaningful? Er . . .

The Tourists – Reality Effect (courtesy Logo Records)

RECORD SLEEVE SLEAZE

Respected rock writer Charlie Gillett is the prime mover and figurehead of a small record label called Oval (named after Kennington Oval in London, presumably, as Charlie lives in that vicinity). On a couple of occasions, Oval has attempted to expand by allowing its distribution etc., to be performed by a major label, but thus far, these moves have met with little apparent success. During 1979, Oval was briefly affiliated with A & M Records, and perhaps the brevity of that relationship can be pratically explained by the album sleeve pictured here, which shows with some clarity that to allow an artist to appear as an album sleeve can be a definite risk. While slightly preferable to yet another naked nubile nymph, Shrink's sleeve was hardly likely to convince casual browsers that, even at the reasonable price of £1.59 for a six track ten inch record, their life would be immeasurably enriched if they invested in the disc it contained.

Shrink – Shrink (courtesy of A&M/Oval – Photo Andra Nelki)

Only one artist can boast two sleeves on which he features being selected for this ghoulish gallery, and it's perhaps surprising to note that the artist, Al Kooper, is in fact an extremely talented and highly rated musician. Kooper played with Bob Dylan, founded two successful bands (The Blues Project and Blood, Sweat and Tears), and nowadays is an in demand record producer, having worked with The Tubes, Lynyrd Skynyrd (a band he also discovered), Eddie and the Hot Rods and David Essex, among others. The title of the first (and best) LP by Blood, Sweat and Tears, *Child Is Father To The Man*, features all eight band members standing or sitting with child-sized facsimiles of themselves. Pretentious but passable. Somewhere, though, the execution has gone sadly awry. The lighting and general colouration is so lurid that the overall effect is that of a freakshow. Far worse, though, is the sleeve to Kooper's 1976 solo LP, *Act Like Nothing's Wrong*. While the airbrush artist who produced the finished man's-head-on-a-woman's-body, woman's-head-on-a-man's-body pictures cannot be faulted, his final end product cannot have won him too many friends.

Blood Sweat and Tears

Taste is not a word which Bad Manners would connect with anything other than various varieties of refreshment (as in 'here, I can hardly taste the whisky'), but the sleeve to their second, and highly successful, album, *Loonee Tunes* can hardly be judged to have broadened the boundaries of good taste, although they have done precisely the reverse for bad taste. But did they have to take advantage of what appears to be a splendid example of a man's best friend? And did they make the dog eat something unpleasant to produce this nauseous puddle?

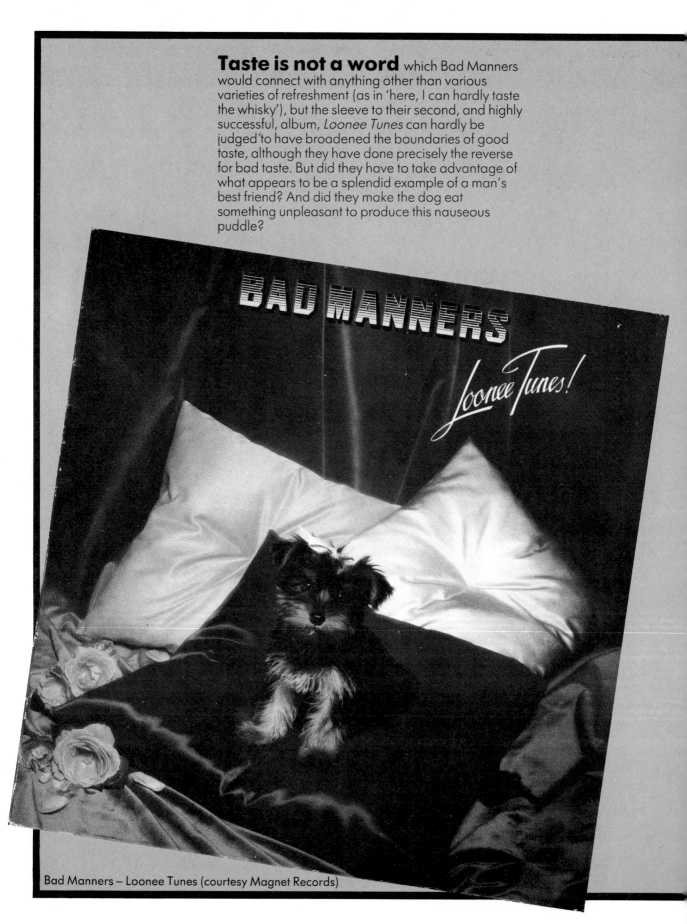

Bad Manners — Loonee Tunes (courtesy Magnet Records)

Jonathan King and Friend

Elsewhere, the subject of decorating

your sleeve with a mutant man has been discussed, and similar popularity seems to have been enjoyed by depicting blood leaking from a limb. Not as the result of some violent disagreement, mind you, which would be disgusting enough in the manner of Oxfam posters (although infinitely less useful), but as a result of some mild kind of self-mutilation.

Three particular LPs come to mind, the first being by Jonathan King, the media personality and sometime owner of his own record label, who has also enjoyed a string of hit records over the years, often under various bizarre pseudonyms such as One Hundred Ton and A Feather, Bubblerock and The Weathermen. King's contribution to the self-abuse stakes came on his 1975 LP, *A Rose In A Fisted Glove*, the title of which may supply a clue as to the detail pictured on the sleeve – a white gloved hand grasps the stalk of a rose on the front, while on the rear, the rose has been dropped and the white gloved hand opened to display three large spots of blood. The album itself is

the usual King melange of the inspired and the totally banal, although another King LP, *Try Something Different* contains the ultimate piece of King kitsch in his alarming version of the Dionne Warwicke/Aretha Franklin hit, *I Say A Little Prayer*. As the artist himself describes it on the sleeve: "A chorus of gay Spanish monks, castanets at their fingertips, chant in Latin, and we're away". He fails to mention that the song is specifically designed to be sung by the female of the species (or at least it was at the time it was written), so that lines like 'The moment I wake up, before I put on my make up' or 'Back combing my hair now, and wondering what dress to wear now' sound as though they are being sung by a transvestite at the very least. The climax of the song when Jonathan and the 'gay monks' are subjected to constantly rising key changes which they find more and more difficult to sustain brings the whole thing to a horrific conclusion. This track is in fact only marginally superior in the depths it plumbs to a version of *Mr. Tambourine Man* (one of the tracks on which King masquerades as Bubble-rock), accompanied, but of course, by a band of fifteen tambourine players.

The last thing which Jonathan wants to convey most of the time is gravity or consequence, and the same is true of the sole LP made by the strange duo, Yin and Yan, whose LP sleeve features two people shaking hands with each other, once again, clasping a rose, this time between both hands, which are naturally dripping blood. Yin and Yan were in reality Chris Sandford, an actor who once enjoyed a starring role in the British TV soap opera *Coronation Street* during the 1960s, and Bill Mitchell, also an actor, but in addition a noted impersonator and the possessor of an exceedingly deep voice. The album's major raison d'etre was a humorous cover version of the song *If*, which itself had become a number one hit during the early part of 1975 – the Yin and Yan spoof occurred later that same year. Although much of the record is intentionally and at times genuinely funny, the duo occasionally lacked the benefit of objective quality control, as a short non-musical sketch with the unlikely title of *Condom* unfortunately proved – it was neither outrageous nor funny, thus to some extent destroying the point of making the record in the first place. The version of *If* which Yin and Yan were mocking was not, by the way, the 'serious' version of the song by Bread,

Yin and Yan – Tales For Heads (courtesy E.M.I. Records)

but a bizarre monologue by Telly 'Kojak' Savalas, at the time at the peak of his popularity as a lollipop sucking New York policeman. We will no doubt be mentioning Telly's contributions to musical mayhem at some other point . . .

The third of the protagonists in this particular drama are a duo who call themselves Suicide. This in itself is hardly furthering the cause of good taste, although Alan Vega and Marty Rev, the two New Yorkers who took the name, have justified the choice in their own minds thus: "We were sitting in a room with all these junkies, and suddenly the name came. We looked around this room and there were all these artists, jazz heads and great painters, this and that, writers, and they're all sitting just shooting up, trying to off themselves."

Suicide's music is certainly among the most stark and dramatic you may ever hear, with Vega whispering, wailing and screaming into his microphone and Rev, the sole instrumentalist in the band, playing keyboards and operating an electronic drum machine. However, due to the fact that the group first attracted attention during the early and often violent

Suicide

days of punk rock, added to which they frequently played as support act to major stars with almost messianic followings unwilling to tolerate anything but their own particular favorite, their performances were often abbreviated to as little as ten minutes due to the constant hail of missiles and abuse hurled at them by impatient and lemming like audiences. One might reasonably feel that while the duo were prepared initially to tolerate the physical and verbal abuse to which the vast majority of audiences subjected them, they would be looking forward to a time when they were sufficiently established to become the recipients of praise, but when I phrased a suggestion to that effect to Marty Rev, he was rather less eager for normal appreciation than might be imagined: "Being applauded can be strange — it depends where, and the kind of applause, because that can be deceptive and a little stifling. I think it's inevitable that we would have to disenfranchise ourselves from the public again, otherwise we'd lose a certain amount of validity — we tend to feel that we're saying something with that kind of negative reaction we receive."

Of course, should either Marty or Alan suffer anything more serious than the cuts, lumps and scratches which they have come to expect as the normal repercussions of their performance, that attitude might change drastically . . .

Returning to the point after that somewhat longer than normal detour, the second Suicide LP is contained in a striking sleeve — the front is vaguely disturbing without anything being specifically recognizable, but the rear shows a presumably female leg being shaved with what is normally termed a safety razor. In this case the epithet seems inaccurate, as the razor has removed a significant chunk of flesh, leaving a bleeding aperture. Very Gothic . . .

Subtlety seems to have been the idea of the Suicide sleeve, especially when it is compared with a celebrated album cover to be found on *Weasels Ripped My Flesh* by Frank Zappa and the Mothers Of Invention. A smiling caricature of a business man is dragging across his cheek a small rodent which appears to be electric, as it has a power lead issuing from its rectum. Both the claws and the teeth of the animal are inflicting substantial damage on the tender flesh of the business man, who nonetheless continues to smile, albeit with a somewhat odd expression on his face . . .

ALL YOU NEED IS HYPE - promotion and advertising

1980 saw the frontiers of rock

outrage extended by a considerable distance, with the evolution of a New York band who called themselves The Plasmatics. The first we heard of this genuinely grotesque group was a review of one of their 'concerts' which took place at a club somewhere in that hyperactive city, and what follows are extracts from what was published: "The Plasmatics put the puke in punk. It's ersatz and exploitation in overdrive, yet The Plasmatics actually pride themselves on being the most vile, worthless group of scum-mongers around. Lead singer Wendy Orleans Williams spends most of the show fondling her family size breasts, scratching her sweaty snatch, and eating the drum kit, among other playful events".

The same writer observed that there was nothing particularly original about the band (a good reason, presumably, for avoiding the United States if one wishes to go out for a quiet drink and not be confronted with a Wendy O. Williams-shaped apparition). However, anyone attempting to write The Plasmatics off as boring sleaze seemed to be missing the point, and the group created an almost unhealthy aura of expectancy, fuelled by the frequent appearance of pictures of Ms. Williams, bare breasted save for a pair of strategically placed strips of black insulating tape across her nipples.

The Williams life story then began to emerge via various feature stories about her group in the music press. After a relatively normal childhood and a certain amount of teenage globetrotting, Wendy migrated to New York to become . . . (and here Ms.

Williams takes up the story herself). "I will do anything as long as there is a certain *quality* involved. The shows I was in were like the fucking Cadillacs of sex shows. It was all costumed, choreographed and scripted – I was cast like a dominatrix, a strong female character. I liked it being slightly illegal – I was arrested over a hundred times and I loved it! There was nothing sleazy about the shows. It wasn't just a girl walking on stage and fucking. It wasn't that kind of show – there was never a guy and a girl fucking in these shows".

At this point, Wendy was interrupted by the group's manager, who noted: "I don't know why she's saying that there weren't guys and girls fucking on stage, because there were". Wendy: "In the last couple maybe. It wasn't the main constituent of the show". Manager: "Yeah, there was an emotional build up to it, which was why there was standing room only . . . But Wendy's speciality was in the girl-to-girl numbers. She did perform hard-core sex, but not with men on stage. It was as hard as you can get. Oral sex, penetration with . . . anything."

Then the aforementioned manager decided that there was more money to be made in music, and the kind of publicity already mentioned began to flood the media. "Wendy O. Williams, the girl who has made love onstage seventeen hundred times", along with quotes like "I am a blatant exhibitionist and I always wanted to be a rock 'n' roll singer. Now that I've got the opportunity, I've never had so much fun in my life, and I've never had so many orgasms in my life

Plasmatics – New Hope For The Wretched
(courtesy Stiff Records)

– my panties are always wet". In fact, this could be seen as a false step – did this sex bomb wear underwear? What a let down!

A group was assembled around Ms. Williams, although the great majority of critics made it clear that three of the four other musicians in the band were paid strictly to do what they were told. The exception was guitarist Ritchie Stotts, whose onstage costumes were bizarre to say the least – sometimes he appeared as a nurse, but mostly his stage wear included a corset, suspender belt and nylons with a ballerina's tutu, the whole ensemble being nicely set off by his blue dyed Mohican haircut. It should be noted here that this kind of horror comic look failed to upset Stott's parents, although Mr. Stott Senior did chide Ritchie thus: "Son, did you really have to cross your eyes like that in those photographs?"

There can be no doubt that a certain element of

exaggeration permeated much of this publicity – or so everyone in Britain thought, until eye-witnesses returned from New York with first hand descriptions, such as the one which follows, by Phil Sutcliffe in the music magazine *Sounds*.

"Mental processes aborted as a thousand pairs of hands erupted from the P.A. The man to blame first off was Ritchie Stott, who seemed to be performing open-heart surgery on his guitar without the benefit of anaesthetic. It was screaming ... And there was Wendy O. Williams swinging a sledge hammer to fragment a couple of radios which had been set up for our entertainment by a passing member of the Ku Klux Klan. She grabbed a mike and started to bawl. This must have been a song.

"What happened was Wendy hammered a TV to bits, blasted a few amplifiers and brought down a section of the lighting rig shooting a sawn-off shotgun from the hip, and took an amplified chainsaw to a couple of guitars, all the while vigorously rubbing her crotch as if she only wished she had a power sander so she could do the job properly. The band played maximum speed maximum noise, colored by the blood of Ritchie Stott who was biffing himself around the head with his guitar. Wendy teased the smouldering fuses of sticks of 'dynamite' over her body as if they reminded her of something less potent, then lobbed them into the shining red car. Three miked up explosions axed our skulls. The last one flipped the bonnet off and blew a ball of fire fifty feet into the air. Then she destroyed a few more amps with her shotgun, the base player 'hung' himself, and the show was over. No encores".

After a build up (not to mention wind up) of this nature, the appearance of some kind of vinyl proof of the pudding was awaited with a certain expectancy, although with rather less excitement than the news that this remarkable stage show would be seen on a London stage (although there was some doubt as to how much of the mutilation and destruction would be tolerated by the Greater London Council, and fortunately for the credibility of the record company who had organized the British tour, this was openly expressed). The first Plasmatics record to be released was indeed a damp squib. Wrapped in a predictably tacky picture sleeve, which showed Wendy sawing a guitar in half with her chainsaw, taped nipples well to the fore, and with Ritchie Stotts wearing a rapist's mask, *Butcher Baby* was nothing more than a terrible noise with very few redeeming features other than

qualities which made it a certainty to be mentioned in the book you are reading.

During August, 1980, the band arrived in Britain, and were scheduled to perform at London's Hammersmith Odeon. Stiff Records claimed that they had supplied full details of the carnage which the Plasmatics would be perpetrating some weeks before, but four hours before the gig was scheduled to commence, the GLC insisted that almost all of what were termed 'special effects' must be dropped, and eventually decided that the performance could not take place. At a press conference next day, Wendy O. Williams 'justified' her group's position thus: "Violence, destruction, sex – it's always been a part of rock 'n' roll. And it's not up to a bunch of fifty year old, monkey-brained fascist farts to tell *us* what we're going to do". Ritchie Stotts added "The GLC said they'd bend over backwards to allow the chainsaw to go through the guitar. But the chainsaw's part of our music. It's on the record."

Somewhat miffed by this setback, The Plasmatics returned to America, where it was decided that they should further fuel the publicity fire by what they termed 'a statement on American consumerism, – Wendy would drive a Cadillac without any brakes into a stage loaded with explosives. If she failed to bail out of the car in time, manufacturers of chainsaws, explosives and insulating tape would be forced into mourning, but whatever happened, it was alleged that twenty thousand dollars would be kissed goodbye as a result of this distasteful stunt. Several hundred people (described by a reporter as "decidedly unattractive") were there to watch the event, which was also covered live by two television stations. After a thirty-minute 'performance' on the stage, Wendy climbed into the car which moved at a sedate 15 miles per hour towards the now vacated stage. Inevitably, and perhaps unfortunately, she managed to jump out before the car ploughed into the powder keg, which exploded dramatically, and was then pushed into the Hudson River by the car, which also met a watery grave.

The world is now holding its collective breath in anticipation of fresh and even more senseless destruction, although it seems that The Plasmatics have to a large extent destroyed their credibility by releasing a debut LP which found favor with several critics. One reviewer wrote: "I must confess to being initially surprised by just how well the record stands on its own merits, deprived as it is of the baying of salivating hordes and the death cries of sacrificial automobiles. This is a slice of classic plastic"

What a disappointment! This, of course, firmly negates the top secret CIA plan to drop Wendy O. Williams behind the Iron Curtain, where a few minutes of one of her shows would be guaranteed to send the entire population of the USSR screaming towards China, resulting in a large portion of South East Asia sinking into the sea.

THESE STICKERS WERE ISSUED

to the staff at EMI Records during the same week as the industry giant (read dinosaur) was taken over by Thorn Electrical Company. Shortly afterwards, numerous redundancies were announced – hopefully among them was the person responsible for formulating the wording on the stickers, which were mostly used by redundant staff to deface the company's property.

WHEN THE SEX PISTOLS' SINGLE 'GOD Save The Queen' was released by Virgin Records during the week when Britain was celebrating the Queen's Jubilee, and despite rarely being played on the radio, and not being stocked by many of the most powerful record stores, the single entered the chart at number eleven, and finally rose to number two in the British charts. A boat trip on the River Thames was organised by manager Malcolm McLaren to celebrate this breakthrough, but this also ended in chaos and police activity after fighting broke out on board, following which several members of the group's entourage were arrested.

THE LETTER REPRODUCED HERE WAS sent to numerous media persons presumably as an attempt at the kind of subtle (read 'disgustingly fawning') approach which might result in a record being mentioned in the press or played on the radio. It was obviously intended as a joke, but the real joke seems to be that neither the author of this book, nor anyone else in the media, seems to have played the record. But as a publicity stunt, it perhaps wasn't such a bad idea, particularly the stuff about the pigeon.

c/o Nudge Nudge Records,
14 Castle Road,
Kentish Town,
London, NW1.

Dear Sir/Madam/God-like being who holds in his omnipotent grasp both the singular and collective futures of myself, my wife, my seventy-three children, thirteen concubines, twelve whippets, nineteen gerbils, fifteen squatters, apoplectic bank manager, landlord, publican, bookmaker, social security officer and transcendental psychoanalist – not to mention the various and nefarious well-built gentlemen who are constantly ringing my doorbell, only to discover that I am 'not in'. . .

Here is a record. My record. MUSCLE AND MONEY.

Give it a whirl.

Should it move you to look down with kindness from the Olympian Heights, then we, the above, shall be eternally grateful; Yea, even unto the Nth generation. And I personally pledge to sacrificially slaughter a fatted wildebeeste in your name every third Wednesday in the month, when it falls on a full moon.

On the other hand, should you consider it to be the most loathsome abomination to ever crawl, stinking from the Primeval Slime – then simply punch out the centre of the record, pop it over the head of the enclosed carrier pigeon and hurl both through the nearest available window.

Yours Fawningly,

P.S. A word of warning: Please open this letter carefully. We are experimenting with a breed of genetically mutated carrier pigeon which tends to be a bit quick off the mark. Hence we have received complaints from people who have found no pigeon enclosed with this letter – merely a few feathers and smattering of guano.

Thank You.

Malcolm McLaren (c. Jill Furmanovsky)

ALL YOU NEED IS HYPE

Connie and the Cocksuckers

is regarded with some suspicion, although it must be admitted that this is often completely unjustified – for every chunderer one meets in the vicinity of Earl's Court, there are at least a dozen very pleasant relatives of convicts. In this particular section, however, we shall see that any impression of the Australian nation in general, and their rock music scene in general, as tasteless beyond belief, may very well be totally justified.

Firstly, the advertisement which appeared in RAM magazine for Rev. John Heinous and the Rancid Virgins during November 1979 is unfortunately totally self-explanatory. The fact that this ad mentions the group's 'latest blatent atrocity' must lead to some conjecture about what preceded it, which we are happily not in a position to reveal . . . Next, a sweet all female band rejoicing in the name of Connie and the Cocksuckers. What is most interesting here is that the advertisement fails to mention any record these ex-debutantes may have made, although readers are enjoined to send away for further (and presumably larger) copies of the poster.

Next up (no doubt following your lunch) come The Clingers, described by a salivating copy writer as 'Soft bodies, hard rock'. These ladies appear to have avoided any contact with the women's liberation movement – perhaps they might have found it difficult to burn their foundation garments, as it would appear that they were little interested in owning such clothes.

Reverting to that subtlety for which many Australians are noted, we come to a picture described by the rock historian who supplied it in the following terms: "Multi-platinum Australian group 01' 55 in a publicity print taken in 1977, which was banned before issue. Saxophonist Wilbur Wilde (now with Jo Jo Zep and the Falcons) displays that legendary Australian nocturnal animal, the white eared elephant".

Soft Bodies.
Hard Rock.

OL'55

One of the methods used by record

companies at least theoretically, to peddle their wares more effectively is the press reception. These occasions are sometimes comfortably predictable – the invitees, a hundred or more media people, are greeted at the door of a venue specially chosen and hired for the occasion. These 'guests' sit down and proceed to eat and drink as if there were no tomorrow. The refreshments, being quite free, are regarded as a singular boon by a certain percentage of the assembled media, who have little money and might starve were it not for their having been invited. After an hour or so of Bacchanalian revelry, the act in whose honor the reception is being thrown (read 'the act whose new record has just been released') may play a generally uninspired series of selections from their new product.

This, then, is the format of the run of the mill reception. From time to time, however, when a record company feels particularly generous (read 'has spent so much money on making the record that it needs to sell millions of copies merely to break even'), a plane load of key media personnel (read 'friends of the person responsible for the invitations') may be flown to some remote part of Europe for the unveiling of the record (read 'to hear it played impossibly loudly on studio equipment which could make The Osmonds sound like The Beatles'). Sometimes, of course, these occasions, despite their less than altruistic intentions, are actually highly enjoyable – one such was the launch party for the then new Rocket Records label, co-owned by Elton John and his manager, John Reid. Several hundred liggers (a 'ligger' is one prepared to accept hospitality without any promise of returning it in kind) boarded a special train at Paddington Station in London for a mystery destination, which turned out to be the picturesque Moreton-in-the-Marsh in Gloucestershire. The train was loaded with an inexhaustible supply of alcoholic beverages, and one of its coaches has been transformed into a discotheque. These facilities helped to pass the time splendidly until the train reached its destination. On arrival, the semi-inebriated company were met by a brass band, who conducted the guests to a medieval dining hall where a Falstaffian array of comestibles was eagerly consumed, thrown, ground into the floor. A brief performance by one or two of Rocket's initial signings followed by a jam session led by Elton John concluded the proceedings and the bedraggled crowd wandered back to the train for the return journey. All very pleasant, but the cost must have been enormous.

And then come the less successful receptions.

One such took place during the first half of the 1970s, the occasion being the presentation to Argent, a band of that era, of some gold or silver records for sales in some part of Europe. For no good reason that could be ascertained, the presentation was to take place in a club in Wolverhampton, without doubt one

VERY FEW PEOPLE

ever seem to have heard Keep The Dogs Away, *the first LP by an object called Thor. Having seen this advertisement, they presumably couldn't listen for laughter.*

of the least impressive towns in Britain in the eyes of the London media. However, 'surprises' were promised in addition to the expected alcoholic excess, the first of these being a coach with ablution facilities to ease the problem of having to stop at each motorway service area for bladder evacuation. In order that these facilities should be given the chance to function freely, a 'lady' was hired to dispense the refreshments from a Topless Waitresses Agency – the person whose job it was to make the arrangements was somewhat surprised that the bill for the waitresses services had to be settled in advance, and included Value Added Tax!

According to eye witness reports, the lady was apparently topless in more ways than one — she was certainly wearing nothing on the upper half of her body, but as her chest seemed to resemble that of a small boy, any 'surprise' quotient seemed to be lacking. Upon the party's eventual arrival at the club, the drunken bunch were shown into a private bar while the club's normal business, that of a discotheque, continued as usual. Shortly before midnight, the by now exceedingly inebriated media were dragged away from their drinks to watch the event for which the entire outing has been organized. However due to a combination of the club being excessively crowded and the inability of most of the London party to either stand up or focus their eyes, very few of those who had been transported to see this less than momentous presentation were conscious that it had occurred. At this point, the club was emptied of its normal clientele, and the stumbling media assembled into a group, save for one national newspaperman who, it later transpired, had checked into the local hospital, fearing that he was suffering from alcoholic poisoning as he had encountered the symptoms previously.

When the club was devoid of normal paying customers, the doors were locked (!), and the last of the 'surprises' was announced — blue lights illuminated the now nearly empty club (only the coach party remained). "Gentlemen" intoned an unpleasant individual, who claimed to be the Manager of the act which was about to perform. "please keep your drinks in your left hand, because you'll need your right hands for wanking. Unless, of course, you're left-handed . . ." At this, enormously unsubtle striptease type music played and two well-built females in their thirties paraded on stage, and proceeded to remove their own and each other's clothing. This was followed by a certain amount of titillation directed at the few persons in the small audience who were still marginally conscious, and this was apparently the point when a television director broke two ribs in a vain attempt to ravish one of the performers. The, uh, climax of the entertainment came when a record company A & R man, who needed little encouragement to participate, was ravished simultaneously by both performers, and then encouraged to intercourse. At this stage, reports differ — some witnesses suggest that despite his high level of arousal, the A & R man was too drunk to be capable; others reckon that he was fellated to a halt. It was, by this time, close to dawn and the survivors struggled back to the coach, where the topless waitress refused to bare her non-existent chest on the grounds that (a) it was too cold, and (b) she had only been contracted for the outward trip. However, the

Elton John

general feeling of the party was that it made very little difference, as most were feeling too ill for anything other than the Third World War to make a significant impact. The final score, then, was one hospitalized, one with rib injuries and about twenty with severe hangovers.

But what finally made the entire episode totally pointless was that the film taken of the presentation to the group was never used, and common decency made it impossible for any of the journalists concerned to report the occasion. The group, fortunately or unfortunately (for they had apparently approved the idea behind the event), broke up quite soon afterwards, and hundreds of pounds were wasted by the record company, who paid for the coach, enough alcohol to stock a good-sized off-licence, the topless waitress, the 'floor show', plus, conceivably the hospital bills of the casualties. It is indeed fortunate that such 'receptions' are few and far between . . .

ONE OF THE LESS TASTEFUL

pranks played by record pluggers (or promotion executives, as they prefer to be called) on radio stations deserves a spot (as in blemish) in this book. A smiling plugger arrived at the stations with a box of gleaming yellow T-shirts, accompanied by a press release which read: "We are thrilled to reveal the signing of L. A. Band and Uncle Sherman. The group have loomed large on the L. A. club scene for several months, and their outrageous act has caused considerable excitement. Uncle Sherman were finally clinched after a free concert in Venture Park, California, when hundreds of girls were overcome by the group's zippy performance. The first Uncle Sherman release will be Expose, which, due to its length, will be available as a 12" only". The T shirt, by the way, was decorated with a picture of a middle aged man wearing a raincoat, part of which flapped upwards to reveal the gentleman's most prized possession. Re-reading the press release revealed more than just the joke . . .

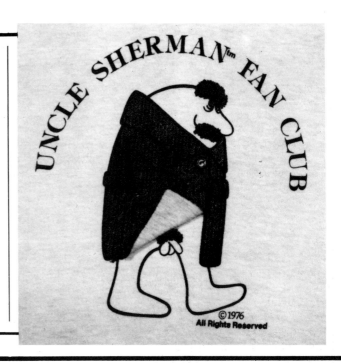

The Royal Family

DID THE PEOPLE

who conceived of dubbing this rather average sextet The Royal Family really think that anyone would be fooled? Even the names of the group were suspect, if in some cases, not completely impossible – Tudor Royal and Rob Royal: well, perhaps. Roger King: definitely. Charlie Prince: come on, now. Mick Kent: as in Duke of, presumably? Keith Constantine: of Greece, perhaps? The group, you may well have guessed, vanished without trace, indicating that there is still some justice in the world . . .

FREE MONEY FREE PRIZES

WE HERE AT SATELLITE WOULD LIKE TO SEE THIS SINGLE 'CHARTING SHORTLY'

In order to meet our sales target we are offering many wonderful 'favours' to anyone able to help our product to the NUMBER ONE POSITION

FREE MONEY FREE PRIZES

WE HERE AT SATELLITE WOULD LIKE TO SEE THIS SINGLE 'CHARTING SHORTLY'

In order to meet our sales target we are offering many wonderful 'favours' to anyone able to help our product to the NUMBER ONE POSITION

AMAZE YOUR FRIENDS

SUPER BACK HANDERS

GIFTS FREE

FREE
Four Talbot Sunbeams for every 300 ticks in the BMRB chart return book.

FREE
Edinburgh Castle for every five plays on daytime Radio One.

FREE
Your very own Inter-City 125 for every hour long interview with Michael Parkinson.

SEE BACK FOR FURTHER DETAILS

John Lydon   Public Image Ltd   Virgin Records

Public Image Limited

FOLLOWING THE EXCESSES

of his first group, the Sex Pistols, it might be thought that John Lydon (the name to which Johnny Rotten reverted, at least in his own mind, although the media seem relatively unaware of the change) would have attempted to avoid anything which might be termed controversial. However, his new band, Public Image Ltd., seemed to change its drummers as often as Johnny reportedly cleaned his teeth (three times a year?), and by 1981, the 'group' was reduced to Lydon singing, original guitarist Keith Levane (who, much earlier, had been sacked by the original Clash) plus a lady named Jeannette Lee, whose role in the band appeared to be mysterious, to say the least, as she seemed not to play any musical instrument nor to sing. Prior to this depletion an early product of Public Image Ltd. was the notorious Metal Box – this artefact consisted of a round flat can, such as is used for transporting film, inside which were three twelve inch 45 r.p.m. records. Fair enough – except that removal of the discs was extremely difficult, as the records were only a millimetre or two smaller than the box, added to which they were not encased in a normal inner sleeve, but merely separated by a thin piece of paper, resulting in almost inevitable damage. For reasons which have never been satisfactorily explained, Lydon and his band instructed their record company that no promotional copies of the Metal Box should be sent out, although the vast majority of those who have heard them consider that the records contained in the box, with or without the damage caused by removing them from their covering, are hardly worth the trouble of switching on your hi-fi. It may be interesting to note that the group's American record company would have none of this foolishness, and insisted that the records were packaged in a conventional sleeve. This did not prevent a riot breaking out when the group played a date in a New York theater, after PIL insisted on playing behind the large video screen . . .

One of the more unlikely, and oddly

enough, partially successful publicity stunts ever perpetrated in the field of pop music occurred in 1972, when a London revival band known as The Rock 'n' Roll Allstars apparently needed a shot in the arm to boost their flagging career. To achieve this, someone suggested that the band should somehow contrive to perform in Communist China, and it must be charitably supposed that in fact some efforts were made to achieve the necessary permission to extend the frontiers of popular music to an area in which the genre was unknown. Predictably enough, there was no way that Chairman Mao (or at least those to whom he delegated this type of responsibility) was going to allow any Western musicians (let alone a band who, with the best will in the world were hardly even vaguely famous beyond certain parts of South London) to bring the dreaded capitalist message to his territory.

This seemed to be the end of the whole scheme, until the group's publicist, who had somewhat optimistically already embarked on a saturation publicity campaign based around the projected tour, suggested that all would not be lost as long as the band were prepared to spend the best part of six weeks more or less imprisoned in their own homes, seeing no one except their closest relatives and only emerging within sight of the street when curtains were securely drawn. Fired by his enthusiasm, the band agreed to this unlikely plan, and after a lengthy period behind locked doors, emerged blinking into the daylight to

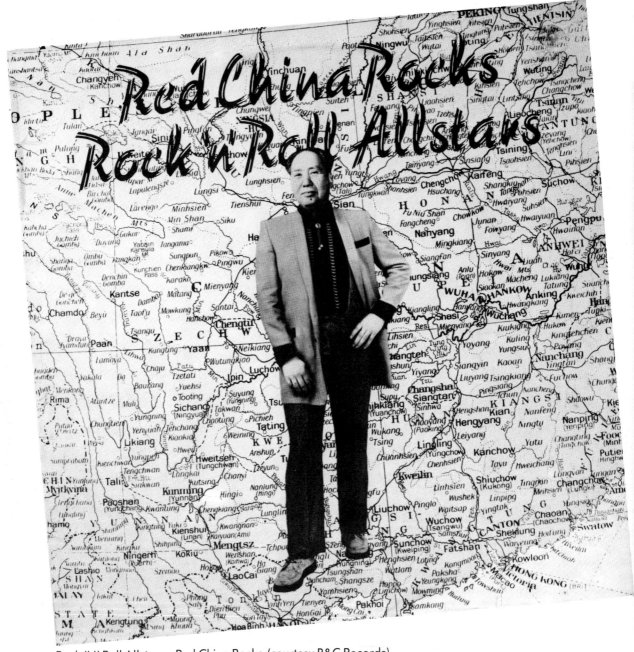

Rock 'N' Roll Allstars – Red China Rocks (courtesy B&C Records)

report on their 'impressions' of China. To compound the felony, as it were, an album was released soon afterwards by the band, titled *Red China Rocks* – much of the sleeve had supposedly Chinese writing on it, while a picture of the band posing in front of a pagoda (possibly in London's Kew Gardens?) while wearing what were presumably supposed to be the kind of clothes worn by Chinese artisans adorned its rear. The head of someone looking a little like Chairman Mao gazed out from the front of the sleeve, although his body appeared to be decked out in Teddy Boy gear, and the whole figure was placed in front of a large map of China. It was all extremely convincing, unless you happened to be familiar with the ruses of the particular publicist working on the band's promotion. After keeping a straight face for some weeks, he eventually broke down in hysterics, admitting that the nearest The Rock 'n' Roll Allstars had been to China was a Chinese restaurant in Tooting. And sure enough, to the left of the Chairman Mao picture on the sleeve, parallel with his right hand, the map of China shows between Chengtu in the North and Kunminf to the South, the ancient Ming settlement of Tooting, London. Although it is not likely that The Rock 'n' Roll Allstars will be remembered for anything else, this one masterly spoof will ensure that their name will not be quickly forgotten.

AS DUBIOUS ADVERTISEMENTS GO, *this one seems to take the biscuit – the occasion occurred following the tragic accident which killed several members of the excellent Southern American group, Lynyrd Skynyrd. The advertisement also shown is perhaps an indication of a slightly more sensitive method of conveying an identical message . . .*

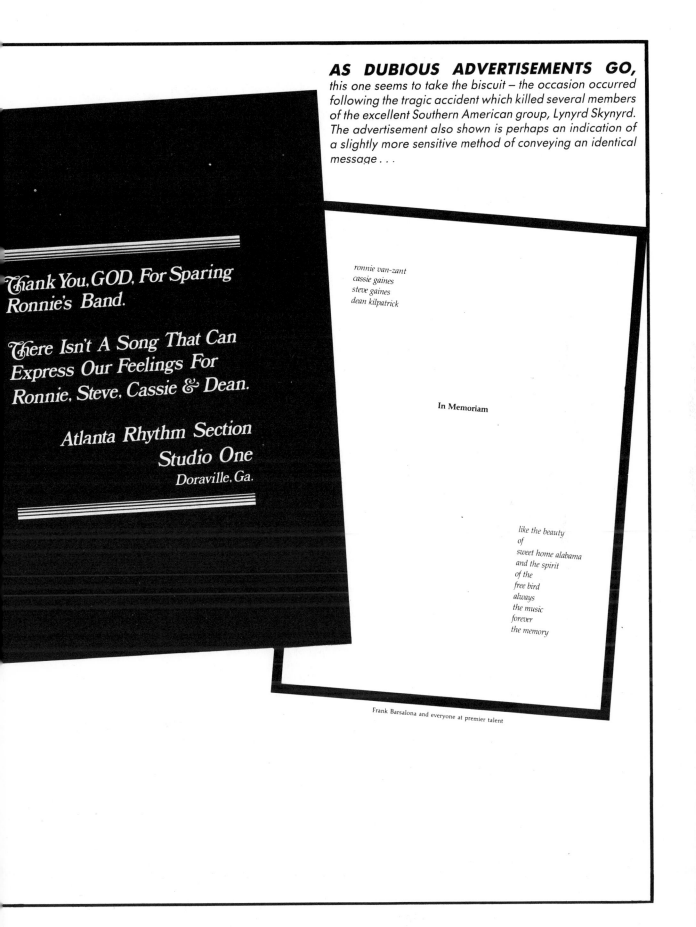

Thank You, GOD, For Sparing Ronnie's Band.

There Isn't A Song That Can Express Our Feelings For Ronnie, Steve, Cassie & Dean.

Atlanta Rhythm Section
Studio One
Doraville, Ga.

ronnie van-zant
cassie gaines
steve gaines
dean kilpatrick

In Memoriam

like the beauty
of
sweet home alabama
and the spirit
of the
free bird
always
the music
forever
the memory

Frank Barsalona and everyone at premier talent

CRUSHED BEATLES - the fab four dismembered

The LP sleeve you see here may not be familiar to the vast number of people who would normally claim that they own every legitimately released Beatle album. It is, you'll agree, a particularly gruesome cover for anything, let alone a record by those lovable mop tops from Merseyside, yet this record was actually released (albeit somewhat briefly) in the United States. According to George Martin, who produced the tracks on the record, he was horrified when he first saw the sleeve, although it has been reported that the Beatles themselves thought the 'concept' was most amusing. Martin, along with other interested parties, tried to apply pressure to have the album withdrawn, which it was shortly after release, and a more conventional 'lovable' sleeve substituted. What is still more interesting is that the LP contains what appears to be a random selection of Beatle tracks with little in common, although sleeve notes indicate that each track is 'rare' in some minor way, such as never having previously been issued in stereo in the US. George Martin also explained the reason for the existence of this, and other similar Beatle collections, which apparently revolves around the differing copyright laws in Britain and America. In the UK, copyright fees are computed per album, regardless of the number of tracks the LP

The Beatles – Casualties (courtesy E.M.I. Records)

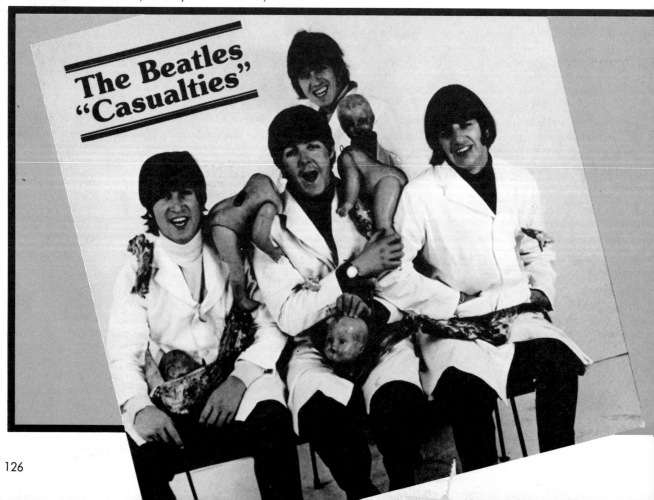

ontains, while the ruling in the United States is that opyright payments are computed for each individual ack. This goes a long way to explaining why American compilation LPs are often very poor value or money, as it is a definite financial disadvantage to ram as many tracks as physically possible onto an album. In the case of the Beatles, their early albums often contained as many as fourteen tracks, which in Britain was considered a bonus, while the group's American record company would usually remove three tracks from the British original in order to 'save' money. These three tracks, together with three more from another album removed for the same reason, plus a few curios, would then be packaged together into an album for release at some future date. This could be marketed as a 'new' Beatle LP – stretching a point without actually telling a lie. The last laugh in this case is on the record company, because the sleeve pictured here came from a bootleg.

One of the more successful ruses

concerning that most famous of all groups, the Beatles, was apparently begun during 1969 by an American magazine which claimed to have incontrovertible proof that Paul McCartney was dead. In evidence, they cited a list of clues which the other members of the group, knowing that the truth would eventually come to light, had inserted in various records. The first of these appeared on the back of the sleeve of *Sergeant Pepper* – Paul is the only one of the four Beatles whose face cannot be seen (although it does, of course, appear quite clearly on the front and in the centerfold of the sleeve, points which were conveniently forgotten in the article). Then there's the booklet which accompanies the *Magical Mystery Tour* soundtrack album – on the penultimate page, where the group are pictured in white tail coats, each of the other three is sporting a red rose in his lapel, while Paul's bloom is black. Turning to the double LP generally referred to as the White Album (though actually called *The Beatles*), if the track *Revolution No. 9* is played backwards, its lyrics apparently contain the phrase 'I buried Paul'. How anyone came to be playing *Revolution No. 9* backwards is one of the great unexplained mysteries of rock! Then comes the conclusive proof – on the sleeve of *Abbey Road*, the group are pictured crossing the road outside their recording studio. John and Ringo, leading the single file procession, are allegedly wearing clothes suitable for mourning. Lennon is in fact wearing a white suit with tennis shoes, not everyone's idea of funeral attire, although Ringo's three piece dark suit with draped jacket and tie might pass muster in a cemetery. Paul, third in line, is barefoot and allegedly dressed for the funeral but he is in fact out of step with the others – he leads with his right foot, while the others lead with

THE MOST OVERPRICED BOOK OF ALL

time must be a volume titled I, Me, Mine, *whose author was ex-Beatle George Harrison. Although it undoubtedly contained some fascinating material, including the original manuscripts of a number of Harrisongs (the name George chose for his publishing company), the price of the leather bound artefact was a mere $250 per copy. Substantial sales, it should be noted, have not been reported . . .*

George Harrison

their left. George Harrison, bringing up the rear, is dressed in the normal working clothes of an English gravedigger. Blue denim shirt, blue jeans, light colored shoes – actually the 'uniform' of just about every male under the age of thirty outside working hours in the Western world. Not a terribly convincing hoax, yet many American Beatle fans believed it implicitly for some time. What was extraordinary, in retrospect, was how quickly the band found a replacement who not only looked exactly like Paul, but who also possessed his amazing songwriting talent.

CARELESS TALK -quotes outrageous and unfortunate

Tiny Tim

John Cooper Clarke: "I've had amnesia for as long as I can remember".

Tiny Tim, the ultimately bizarre singer and ukelele player who scored in the 1960s with ultra camp versions of songs like *Tip Toe Through The Tulips* before vanishing from sight to the relief of all and sundry, was known to utter some peculiar statements. One of the best was: "I think the greatest invention in life is the safety pin, and the second greatest is perfumed toilet paper".

John Cooper Clarke

Kiss

The group Kiss were never noted for their subtle approach to their music – if any member of the audience is able to walk out of the auditorium without ringing ears, the group probably feel that they've had an off night, and even the blood capsules which drip tomato sauce down the jowls of bass playing vampire Gene Simmons and the bullets fired by guitarist Ace Frehley's specially modified instrument to extinguish some stage lights will have been able to do little to lift the crowd. Gene Simmons is also a man who seems to believe in calling a spade a spade: when once asked what he thought about Shakespeare, this modest individual replied: "I think Shakespeare is shit. Absolute shit! He may have been a genius for his time, but I just can't relate to that stuff. 'Thee' and 'thou' – the guy sounds like a faggot. Captain America is classic because he's more entertaining – if you were able to count the number of people who've read something by Shakespeare, you'd be surprised how few it was". It becomes fairly obvious that Gene and John Denver were made for each other . . .

One of the more unlikely personages to make an album was Barbi Benton, whose previous major claim to fame was that she was the live-in girlfriend of Hugh Hefner, founder of the 'Playboy' organization. The unpredictability of life was later expressed by one of her record producers, who noted: "With a pair of tits like that, you tend to forget that she may also have a voice".

Reverting to Australian rockers for a moment, antipodean groups are sometimes rather dismissive about their compatriots, although rarely is an insult so well conveyed as by a member of one Aussie band, The Birthday Party, who was asked to comment on a rival band known as Flowers. "I don't want to talk about them" he said. "It's like tripping up a spastic."

Rube Beard and ZZ Top

During a 1981 British visit, John Cale's observers were somewhat surprised to discover that a small portion of the paying customers were word perfect on a Cale epic titled *Mercenaries (Ready for War)* which was obviously conceived as some kind of anthem. When Cale was asked by a reporter about this song, he said: "It's just a way of exorcising a ghost" – when further pressed as to whether he felt that Armageddon was just around the corner, he said "I wish it wasn't just around the corner, I wish it was here. I don't think anyone can carry out a viable foreign policy with the world under a nuclear umbrella, but if you go through the nuclear barrier . . ." When asked if he found that many people agreed with him on this point, he replied "None".

One of the more heartfelt ambitions among rock 'n' rollers must be that of Z. Z. Top's drummer, Frank Beard, who made the following assertion: "I want the skin of every drum in my kit to have painted on it the face of the first girl I caught crabs from."

Jobriath Boone, an exceptionally pretentious artist from New York, was probably ten years ahead of his time, comprehensively failing to make an impact when his pair of LPs were released in the early '70s. Reportedly, the nearest he achieved to superstardom in Britain was being recognized by a customs official, who suddenly recalled that he had seen Jobriath on the sides of London buses, in the form of advertisements for his debut LP. But maybe the general lack of recognition didn't bother Jo – as he remarked once: "I'm a true fairy".

Rock music seems to revert almost too naturally to bodily functions much of the time. For example, Kevin Ayers is alleged to have said (for no good reason that is discernible), "I have constipated periods, and I find them very depressing". Don't we all, Kev?

Kevin Ayers

CARELESS TALK

Bonnie Raitt, one of the finest female singers ever produced in America, originally rose to prominence to some extent because of her love for the work of pre-war black blues musicians. Whether or not this patronage extended to inviting these old bluesmen to her parties is somewhat more doubtful — as Ms. Raitt once remarked to an assembled gathering: "I don't want to see any faces at this party I haven't sat on". How many accusing looks from her guests can have followed that announcement . . .?

Bonnie Raitt

San Francisco superstars The Jefferson Airplane (later The Jefferson Starship) have experienced continuing personnel upsets during their life span of more than fifteen years, but this turmoil has apparently not affected the sense of humor of members of the band, as evidenced by Spenser Dryden, the band's sometime drummer, who once declared: "What I want to do is run for President of the United States, and then, after I've been elected, I'll set a new trend by assassinating myself". Good luck, Spence . . .

Spencer Dryden (bottom right) of Jefferson Airplane

Joan Baez

The romance between Bob Dylan and Joan Baez must have made the protest movement seem very romantic to some of its followers. But how would they have felt if they had known that some time later, Dylan would reminisce: "She was beautiful in the old days. Used to wipe herself clean with the American flag after doing it". Manufacturers of the Stars and Stripes obviously use very soft material in anticipation of this unlikely use of their product.

Johnny Rotten of the Sex Pistols used to attract attention by stubbing out a cigarette on the palm of his hand during the group's performance, something which later stretched into rolling up his sleeves during the group's appearances to display the scar tissue on his arm from numerous similar cigarette-extinguishing displays. When asked why he performed such a bizarre and painful ritual, Rotten told one journalist: "Pain doesn't hurt (!). I do it for my own amusement, because I think it's going to be fun, and it has nothing to do with anybody else. I won't have people slagging me off for what I do to my own body, because it's *mine*. If I want to cut my own leg off, I will".

Canadian rocker Ronnie Hawkins has always endeavored to bolster his hard-living image but perhaps rarely so graphically as when he reminisced about his love life on the road: "In all that time, I must have laid around a million girls, a few boys and even the odd goat. The goats weren't too bad, except that you had to go around to the other end if you wanted to give them a kiss."

Ronnie Hawkins and Friend

At the start of 1978, The Sex Pistols set
off on their first American tour. A Memphis police chief was obviously preparing for the worst when he allegedly noted: "I don't allow masturbation on stage. They can spit and vomit as much as they like, but no masturbation". At that same show, the group appeared two hours late due to Sid Vicious stabbing himself during the sound check. A few days later, in Texas, Vicious even bettered this stupid prank — after abusing the audience, who in retaliation pelted the group with beer cans, Vicious crowned a member of the audience with his bass guitar. Rotten later told the rest of the audience: "You're a bunch of fucking statues. I've never seen people stand so still in my life. What have you people got between your legs, then?"

Toyah Wilcox

Toyah the British singer, is deter-
mined not to upset her fans, as the following quote will no doubt confirm: "Last night, someone in the audience blew his nose into his hand and then threw the result at me. I had my mouth open at the time, and it went right in. But it's only snot . . ."

The late and generally unlamented
Sid Vicious was another who knew the value of the inflammatory quote. After expressing his distaste for hippies, Sid added: "If I feel like killing one of them one day, I'll do it. I don't need to feel angry to do something like that, because I'm more of a robot than a person." And with a brain to match . . .

Sid and Nancy (c. L.F.I)

Angel

Despite the fact that he has been praised to the skies by writers, Lou Reed is apparently not at all grateful – as he told one interviewer: "Journalists are a species of foul vermin. I wouldn't hire someone like you to guard my sewer. Journalists are morons, ignorant, stupid idiots, and I don't perform for idiots."

One writer who went to see Reed performing, dressed for the gig in a Lou Reed T shirt. A record company employee who was accompanying the journalist said: "That could be a problem – the last writer he saw wearing one of those, he demanded ten dollars from them, because he said he was paying for them anyway". Fortunately, nothing happened to that end. And finally, here's Lou musing on the lyrics of *Waiting For The Man*, some years after he wrote them: "You know, we were rehearsing, running through that song – you know 'Twenty six dollars in my hand' . . . and I said 'Hey, wait a minute, twenty six dollars?' I mean, you can't even get a blow job for twenty six dollars these days, let alone some smack!"

Guitarist Edwin 'Punky' Meadows, who played with a late '70s glitter/heavy metal band known as Angel, may have been listening to the kind of thing which made the Runaways infamous when he told a reporter: "I want a cunt transplant in the back of my guitar so that I can fuck my instrument while I'm playing it". A good exchange for that might be a mouthful of quick setting cement for the silly youth.

Rod Stewart, ex-grave digger of Scottish parentage, probably did wonders for the cause of racial integration when he said: "I think Enoch Powell (the controversial right-wing British MP) has really got it right, and I'm all for what he suggests. Britain is over-crowded, so let's send all the immigrants home as soon as possible, and not allow them back". OK, Rod, your tickets for the trip to your new estate, right next to the Polaris submarine base at Holy Loch, have just arrived . . .

DRUGS AND OTHER JUNK - paraphernalia

In the history of modern popular music,

two names have attracted more attention, more interest and enduring devotion from their fans than any others. One of these, the Beatles, we focus on elsewhere in this book, but the earlier, and probably more revered moniker belongs to Elvis Presley, the deceased but undying king who enjoyed more acclaim and success in the pop music field than any other single person. His overnight rise to fame followed by his virtual seclusion, punctuated by the release of numerous highly forgettable and feeble movies, the vast majority of which were poorly disguised vehicles designed to present Presley to the millions of his fans who might never see him live in performance, paint a sad picture of a talented man unable to escape from the prison into which success placed him.

The stories about Presley are more than legion, a typical example relating to his almost childlike desire to win at whatever game he played. Even when playing Scrabble with his so called friends, a group of his contemporaries known as 'The Memphis Mafia', it is reported that while Elvis allowed himself the traditional number of seven letters with which to make up words, his opponents were only allowed five, thus severely limiting their chances of bettering him. Whether or not there is any truth in stories of this nature is difficult to discern, although they do not, apparently, come as a surprise to those who have attempted an in-depth study of this unhappy man's life.

Remarkable posthumous sales of Presley records (during the week following his death, no less than nine Presley singles appeared in the *British* charts, all but one of them being re-issues) are the key to the horrendous stream of Presley-related merchandise that followed his death in 1977. Much of it is still available today, mostly of questionable value and taste. For instance, a souvenir shop in Nashville, Tennessee, will sell its patrons a selection of dollar bills with Presley's face stuck over what would normally be a picture of George Washington. Despite this defacing, the bills still have printed on them 'This note is legal tender for all debts, public and private', and as they are sold for around five times their face value, it's nice to know that they're good for something.

The same emporium also offers other Presleyana for sale, perhaps the least tasteful artefact being Presley's last will and testament, which can be yours (or, at least, one of a million copies can be yours) for the sum of two dollars. The fact that this document was filed August 22, 1977, a full six days after Presley's demise (although it was purportedly drawn up several months before) may have aroused suspicion in the minds of disbelievers as to the document's authenticity, but it does not seem to have prevented the article from becoming a bestseller.

Perhaps more interesting, to those among us with an appetite for the salacious (ie all of us), is the tale featured recently in a popular newspaper under the headline: 'Elvis' Four Wives'. In essence, the story concerned a trio of ladies, each of whom claimed to have married Elvis Presley some

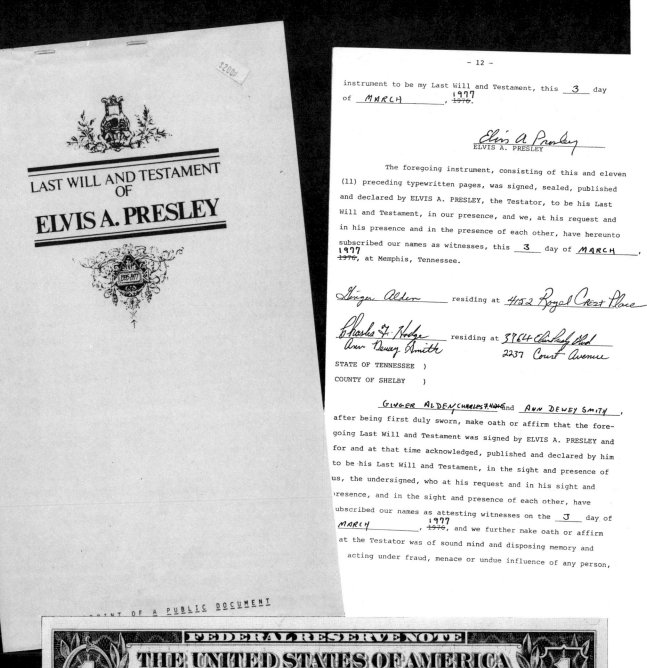

LAST WILL AND TESTAMENT
OF
ELVIS A. PRESLEY

- 12 -

instrument to be my Last Will and Testament, this __3__ day
of __MARCH__, ~~1976~~ **1977**.

Elvis A. Presley
ELVIS A. PRESLEY

     The foregoing instrument, consisting of this and eleven
(11) preceding typewritten pages, was signed, sealed, published
and declared by ELVIS A. PRESLEY, the Testator, to be his Last
Will and Testament, in our presence, and we, at his request and
in his presence and in the presence of each other, have hereunto
subscribed our names as witnesses, this __3__ day of __MARCH__,
~~1976~~ **1977**, at Memphis, Tennessee.

Ginger Alden   residing at __4152 Royal Crest Place__

Charles F. Hodge   residing at __3764 Elvis Presley Blvd__
Ann Dewey Smith   __2237 Court Avenue__

STATE OF TENNESSEE)
COUNTY OF SHELBY)

    __GINGER ALDEN, CHARLES F. HODGE__ and __ANN DEWEY SMITH__,
after being first duly sworn, make oath or affirm that the fore-
going Last Will and Testament was signed by ELVIS A. PRESLEY and
for and at that time acknowledged, published and declared by him
to be his Last Will and Testament, in the sight and presence of
us, the undersigned, who at his request and in his sight and
presence, and in the sight and presence of each other, have
subscribed our names as attesting witnesses on the __3__ day of
__MARCH__, ~~1976~~ **1977**, and we further make oath or affirm
that the Testator was of sound mind and disposing memory and
acting under fraud, menace or undue influence of any person,

PRINT OF A PUBLIC DOCUMENT

ELVIS' FOUR WIVES

I WAS ELVIS' FIRST WIFE

THREE women are desperately competing to be recognized as Elvis Presley's first wife. And none of them is Priscilla, the girl he wed in 1967.

One of the claimants, Billie Jo Newton, says she even gave birth to three of his children, the first when she was only nine years old.

Her incredible story — including marriage at 10 — could not be shaken despite a lengthy GLOBE investigation using lie detectors, hypnosis and voice-stress analysis.

Even so, two other women — Ann Farrell, of Nashville, Tennessee, and Zelda Harris, of Mobile, Alabama — claim they have just as much right to be named the first Mrs. Elvis.

And all three say they have no records of the extraordinary marriages because Presley either ordered the documents to be destroyed or used a fictitious name. He allegedly didn't want his fans to know about any child bride.

If any legal proof emerges, the existence of a first wife and family would threaten the fortune Priscilla and her daughter, Lisa Marie, inherited when Elvis died in 1977.

The three challengers say they have suffered mental anguish because of their secret marriages.

Farrell and Harris were treated in Nashville by psychologist Carlos Herrera who told GLOBE:

● **ANN FARRELL** says she met Presley in 1957 and married him in Russelville, Alabama, a few weeks later.

Herrera says: "She claimed Presley married her because she refused to have sex until they were married.

"Ann said Presley destroyed the marriage license, and all records of the marriage, shortly after."

● **ZELDA HARRIS** says she met Presley during a concert in Mobile, Alabama, after his return from the Army in 1960.

She says they wed within 24 hours, but Elvis was still cautious enough to use a false name because, reports Herrera, "he told her it would be bad for his image as a sex idol if it leaked out he was married."

In the end, Harris adds, he quietly dumped her.

The most convincing evidence of a secret marriage to Elvis comes from **BILLIE JO NEWTON,** 40.

Newton, from Brighton, Tennessee, insists that the superstar divorced her in 1956 on the advice of aides, including his manager Col. Tom Parker.

She claims that marriage records were destroyed. So were the birth certificates of her three children who were taken out of her custody.

Newton told GLOBE that she married Elvis when he was 14. They had been childhood friends and lovers since she was eight.

"That may sound shocking to a lot of people," she says, "but it's not so unusual in the South, especially in rural areas."

During GLOBE's investigation, Newton showed intimate knowledge of Elvis and his family — things known to insiders but never published anywhere.

She told of incidents in great detail and under cross-examination never strayed from her original story.

Newton said it might be difficult getting witnesses to confirm her story because Elvis had bribed them with

'I am not afraid now that he is dead'

gifts to keep quiet.

However, statements from people who knew her and Elvis as childhood friends were verified by GLOBE.

GLOBE arranged for a lie detector test in which an analysis of Billie Jo's voice stress showed that she at least thought she was telling the truth.

years before he married Priscilla Beaulieu, the lady generally regarded as the genuine Mrs Presley. The earliest of these assignations is claimed by the lady involved, Billie Jo Newton, to have produced three children. Newton, who subjected herself to lie detector tests, hypnosis and voice stress analysis in her attempts to have her story authenticated (and this perhaps to row herself into a position where she could claim some portion of the Presley fortune), states that she married Presley when he was fourteen years old, after they had been childhood friends and lovers since she was eight years old. The marriage, claims Billie Jo, took place because she was pregnant, having conceived a child with Elvis when she was nine years old. According to investigators who have questioned her, Ms Newton remembers details concerning Elvis and his family which it would be difficult for anyone other than an 'insider' to recall . . .

The extent of Presley's influence can be further judged by the lady's assertions on the subject of such items as her marriage certificate and the birth certificates of her alleged trio of children. These were said to have been destroyed, and the Tennessee State Registrar confirmed that this was possible, saying: "For a man of Presley's wealth, power and influence in this State, it would not have been difficult at all", a statement which immediately seems to assume even more horrific proportions than anything else in this particular nightmare. Billie Jo has thus effectively sealed off any potential hunt for the alleged children, who she maintains were removed from her custody many years ago, perhaps at the time when this 'marriage' was terminated on the advice of Presley aides, who, in 1956 (the year during which Presley first achieved superstar status) insisted that the couple become divorced.

The women who claim to be Presley's second and third wives have less interesting tales to tell. Ann Farrell's story, that Presley married her in 1957 because she refused to allow him intercourse with her unless they were married, sounds considerably less convincing (a remarkable feat in itself!). Shortly afterwards, continued Farrell, Elvis destroyed all records of the marriage alleged to have taken place in Russellville, Alabama, a claim which might seem to indicate that Elvis could recognize a golddigger when he met one. This might be underlined by Zelda Harris, who reckons that she married Elvis in 1960, following his return from the Army, less than twenty-four hours after the couple met. However, Elvis was smart (or as Harris puts it, 'cautious') enough to use a false name because he told her it would be bad for his reputation as a sex symbol if he were known to be married. Shortly afterwards, in Ms Harris' words, he "quietly dumped" her. This kind of unlikely claim can have done little for the peace of mind of the genuine Mrs Presley, despite the fact that she had herself left Elvis some years before he died, living instead with his karate teacher. The fund of exceedingly unpleasant speculation surrounding the king's private life and times will, no doubt, one day create an industry of its own, by inspiring a soap opera which just might outshine *Dallas*.

Webb Pierce and his Swimming Pool

Webb Pierce and pool

WEBB PIERCE, ACCORDING TO THE details on the reverse of this postcard, "has won more awards for his hit records than any other country singer in the music business". The accuracy of this statement notwithstanding, his construction of a guitar-shaped swimming pool in his back garden still seems a little excessive. .

Papa John Phillips

That flirting with habit-forming

drugs is nothing less than playing Russian Roulette is patently obvious, and that the lives of a growing number of rock stars have been adversely affected, and in some cases, horribly foreshortened is equally clear. It would be foolish to attempt to generalize about the reasons for which musicians become curious about and later addicted to drugs, but as an example of one type of motivation, there follows an extract from Steve Turner's highly recommended book, *Conversations With Eric Clapton*. Clapton has been one of the very fortunate few who, once hooked on heroin, have found the courage and the strength to beat an addiction which at one point developed into a 'habit' which was reportedly costing him up to £1,000 per day. After his cure, Clapton described the effects of heroin thus: "I feel that to be a junkie is to be part of a very elite club, and that's the trouble. Physically, it's just the greatest high you'll ever have. It's like surrounding yourself in pink cotton wool. Nothing bothers you whatever, nothing will phase you out in any way". Turner then writes: 'The fact that most of his idols were junkies and *Layla*, his best album, was made while on heroin spurned him on: "I always argue that all my heroes were junkies – Ray Charles, Billie Holiday, Charlie Parker. They all either die on it, or they're hooked on it. So my argument is that it stimulates your playing – maybe not for long, because sooner or later you hit the downward trail – but for a while it really inspires you."'

And then, of course, unless you're very lucky, it kills you. The list of rock stars which have already been mentioned above as victims contains some enormously inspired and talented people, many of them dead. The needle has claimed these names: Jimi Hendrix, arguably the finest rock guitarist there has ever been; Janis Joplin; Brian Jones, an original Rolling Stone; Al Wilson of Canned Heat; Elvis Presley. Sid Vicious of the Sex Pistols; Malcolm Owen of the Ruts; Ian Curtis of Joy Division . . . and that's only a few of the more famous casualties.

From time to time, however, somewhat in the manner of Eric Clapton, there are rock stars who make valiant attempts to escape from the unhealthy reliance on artificial stimulants. One of the more celebrated recent cases is that of John Phillips, during the 1960s the leader and guiding light of the ultra successful Mamas and Papas, who produced a string of classic hits like *California Dreaming, Monday Monday, Creeque Alley* and *I Saw Her Again*, as well as several million selling albums. During the mid to late years of that decade, the group was virtually second to none in terms of success and popularity. Inevitably, their golden years faded as the marriage between John and his second wife, Michelle, also a member of the group, ended, and although Phillips was no stranger to the drug culture of Hollywood (by this time both the film and rock music center of the Universe), it wasn't until some years later that he became seriously involved in full time addiction. A description of Phillips' physical condition when he finally entered hospital during 1980 was published in 'People' magazine: 'John Phillips was a 45 year old walking cadaver. His 6' 5" frame had shrunk from 210 to 140 pounds. Years of cocaine injections and hits of heroin had killed every vein in each arm up to his elbows. His guitarist's hands were turning black from lack of circulation, and it was feared he would lose the use of them. A blood test sample had to be taken from his neck'. A terrifyingly graphic description . . .

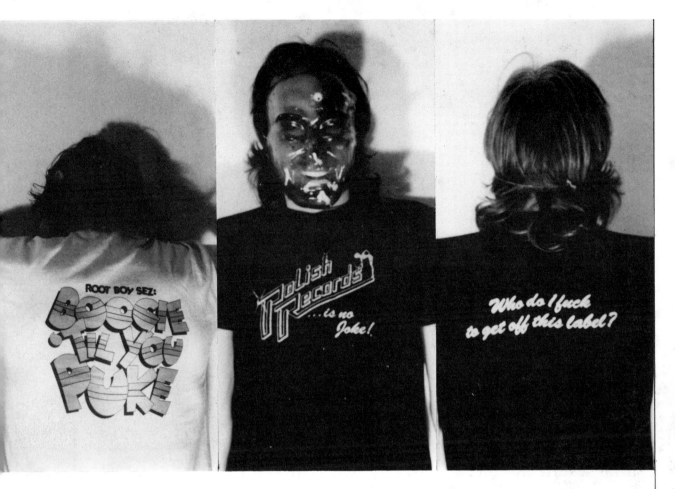

It this were not tragic enough, Phillips' third wife, singer Genevieve Waite, was also totally addicted (it was estimated that Phillips had been spending one million dollars annually on hard drugs to feed his own and his wife's habits), while their new born daughter, Bijou, had only been brought into the world free of the taint of drugs because her mother had been detoxified a few months before her confinement. Added to all this was the fact that Phillips' older daughter, Mackenzie, who had played a major support role in the 1973 nostalgia film success, *American Graffiti*, had also succumbed to drug addiction, and at the age of 21 *People* noted: 'She was already a legend among her Hollywood generation for drug abuse. Colleagues referred to her as "the next Judy Garland". In a year during which Mackenzie spent some three hundred thousand dollars on cocaine, she had lost her job in a TV series, her marriage, and finally almost her life to two overdoses. Mackenzie's brother, Jeffrey, also soon checked into the hospital, where he was apparently swiftly cured, but Phillips' niece, Patty Throckmorton, was less fortunate, and died at the age of 25 from a heroin overdose.

Having embarked on treatment for their addiction (the taking of various non-addictive drugs under strict monitoring — an extreme contrast to the days when John's friend Mick Jagger had to look for him in ultra-sleazy 'shooting galleries', which were described by one doctor as "grungy places with needles on the floor, rats running around and people shooting up with each other's needles"), their troubles are far from over, due to the fact that, at the height of his addiction, Phillips was obtaining stolen prescription forms which he used to acquire drugs for his own family, as well as extra quantities which he would sell to continue to finance his habit. During this period, Phillips calculated that he sold two of his houses, six or seven cars (including four Rolls Royces), valuable paintings, his rights to future record royalties — in short, everything which would turn enough money to buy some more dope.

Such a catalogue of disasters would have been enough to make anyone else lose the will to live. However, John Phillips, to his eternal credit, did not give up the ghost, and despite the fact that he faces a fifteen year prison term plus a twenty five thousand dollar fine, has finally, according to his doctor, discarded his ticket to death. He is also working up to fifty hours per week as a counsellor to other drug addicts, a vocation which Mackenzie also intends to follow. As Phillips says: "It's very hard to make yourself an exhibit, to hold your arm out for people to look at, but I don't want anyone else to go through all the things my family has."